Real English *for*
HOTEL STAFF

실무편 노선희 저

개정판

DARAKWON

Real English *for*
HOTEL STAFF 실무편

지은이 노선희
펴낸이 정규도
펴낸곳 (주)다락원

초판 1쇄 발행 2016년 12월 7일
2판 1쇄 발행 2026년 1월 26일

편집 김태연, 조상익
디자인 김민지, 김예지
영어감수 Michael A. Putlack

다락원 경기도 파주시 문발로 211
내용문의 (02) 736-2031 내선 550
구입문의 (02) 736-2031 내선 250~252
Fax (02) 732-2037
출판등록 1977년 9월 16일 제406-2008-000007호

ISBN 978-89-277-8125-7 14740
     978-89-277-8124-0 14740 (set)

http://www.darakwon.co.kr
다락원 홈페이지를 방문하시면 상세한 출판 정보와 함께 MP3 자료 등의 다양한 어학 정보를 얻으실 수 있습니다.

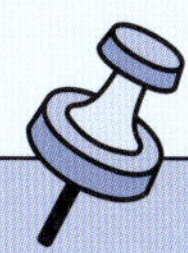

To the Students

　　전 세계 국제관광객 수는 이제 한 해 14억 명이 넘으며 우리나라에도 매년 1,600만 명이 넘는 외국인 관광객이 찾아오고 있습니다. 관광산업의 발전에 따라 호텔산업 분야도 끊임없이 발전을 거듭하고 있습니다. 이러한 시대에 발맞추어 호텔에서는 지원자에게 다양한 자질을 요구하고 있는데, 그중에서도 영어회화 구사 능력은 채용을 결정하는 데 중요한 열쇠가 됩니다. 즉 영어로 자기 생각을 자유롭게 표현하고 의사소통을 원활하게 할 수 있는 능력은 이제 호텔리어의 필수요건이 되었습니다.

　　본서는 고객이 호텔을 예약할 때부터 퇴실할 때까지 관여하는 담당 부서에 따라 순차적으로 단원을 구성하였습니다. 특히 호텔 현장 경험이 없는 예비 호텔리어에게 가장 취약한 부서별 업무 내용을 다양하게 다루어 간접적으로나마 현장 경험을 해볼 수 있도록 하였습니다.

　　본서는 대학의 호텔 및 관광 관련학과 수업교재로는 물론, 호텔 취업 준비생을 위한 독학교재로도 사용될 수 있습니다. 각 단원은 다양한 상황별 대화문과 핵심 표현을 제공하며, 호텔리어와 고객 간 상황극을 연출해볼 수 있도록 롤플레잉 코너도 수록하였습니다. 또한, 매 단원의 마지막 페이지에는 각 호텔 부서를 소개하는 글을 실었으므로 독해 연습과 더불어 호텔 업무 지식을 넓히는 기회로 활용하시기 바랍니다.

　　장차 호텔리어가 될 학생들에게 본서가 유용한 지침서가 되기를 진심으로 바랍니다. 끝으로 본서의 출간을 위해 애써주신 다락원 관계자분들께 깊은 감사의 마음을 전합니다.

2026년 1월

노선희

Contents

Unit	Topic	Objectives	Situations
08	Housekeeping	- Making up Rooms - Other Housekeeping Services	- Making Up rooms - Requesting rooms be made up, turndown service, and other services - Laundry service - Handling lost & found items
09	Hotel Facilities	- At the Business Center - At the Fitness Center	- Photocopy and printing services - Courier and meeting room services - Gyms, saunas, and swimming pools
10	Room Service	- Taking Orders For Room Service - Delivering Room Service	- Taking orders for breakfast - Taking orders for lunch and dinner - Checking orders & delivering room service - Handling mistakes
11	Restaurants & Bars	- Reserving Tables & Greeting Customers - Taking Orders & Handling Payments	- Taking restaurant reservations - Assigning tables to customers with reservations and walk-in customers - Serving at the bar - Taking orders, checking on diners, suggesting desserts, and handling payments
12	Complaints & Problems	- Guest Complaints - Guest Problems	- Complaints about room facilities, mischarges, and wrong rooms - Complaints about restaurant service - Problems with guests' mistakes and room temperatures

NCS 연계 단원 안내

분류체계	능력 단위 및 분류 번호	능력단위요소	연계 단원
직업기초능력 〉 **의사소통능력**	기초 외국어 능력 A-2-마.	외국어 듣기 일상생활의 회화 활용	Unit 01-12
12. 이용 · 숙박 · 여행 · 오락 · 스포츠 〉 03. 관광 · 레저 〉 02.숙박서비스 〉 **02. 객실관리**	객실 예약 접수 1203020201_13v1	객실 및 부대시설 이용정보 파악하기 고객 이력과 기호 확인하기 예약 관련 자료 작성하기 예약 변경하기	Unit 02
	체크 인(Check In) 1203020202_13v1	고객 응대하기 등록카드 작성하기 객실 키 발급 및 정보 제공하기	Unit 04

		고객 요청 사항 처리하기	Unit 04, 08
	재실 고객 관리 1203020203_13v1	객실 변경(Room Change) 하기	Unit 04
		고객 불평 접수하기	Unit 03, 12
	객실 수납 1203020204_13v1	전기(Posting)하기 환전 업무하기	
	체크 아웃(Check Out) 1203020206_13v1	투숙객 정보 확인하기 추가 사용 내역 확인하기 최종 내역 계산하기	Unit 05
		환송하기	Unit 05, 06
	하우스키핑 정비 1203020208_13v1	오더 테이킹(Order Taking) 처리하기 턴다운 서비스하기	
	하우스키핑 관리 1203020209_13v1	호텔 습득물 처리하기(Lost and Found)	Unit 08
	호텔 세탁물 관리 1203020210_13v1	고객 세탁물 접수 처리하기	
12. 이용 · 숙박 · 여행 · 오락 · 스포츠 〉 03. 관광 · 레저 〉 02. 숙박서비스 〉 **03. 부대시설관리**	호텔 레스토랑 서비스 1203020302_13v1	고객 예약 응대하기 고객 영접 및 환송하기 메뉴 추천 및 메뉴 주문 받기 음식 서빙하기	Unit 11
	호텔 음료 서비스 1203020303_13v1	음료 서빙하기	
	식음료 고객 관리 1203020306_13v1	고객 불평 처리하기	Unit 12
12. 이용 · 숙박 · 여행 · 오락 · 스포츠 〉 03. 관광 · 레저 〉 02. 숙박서비스 〉 **05. 접객서비스**	도어 데스크 1203020502_13v1	현관 환대 및 환송하기 발렛 차량 호출하기 택시 호출하기 고객 수하물 전달하기	Unit 03
	벨 데스크 1203020503_13v1	수하물 운반하기 객실 안내하기 고객의 물품 보관하기	
	컨시어지(concierge) 1203020504_13v1	요청받은 정보 제공하기 예약 대행하기 셔틀버스 관리하기 우편물 관리하기	Unit 06
	GRO(Guest Relations Officer) 1203020505_13v1	버틀러 서비스 제공하기	
	귀빈층 라운지(EFL) 1203020504_13v1	귀빈 층 라운지 고객의 체크인, 체크아웃하기 귀빈 층 라운지의 식음료 서비스하기 귀빈 층 라운지의 서비스 안내	
	비즈니스 센터 1203020504_13v1	회의실 관리하기 문서의 복사 및 제본하기	Unit 09
	고객 서비스 센터 1203020508_13v1	내 · 외부의 전화 연결하기 호텔 상품 안내하기	Unit 01
		객실 고객에게 주문받기	Unit 10
		웨이크 업 콜(Wake-up Call)하기	Unit 01

01 Switchboard

Warming Up

A Look at the picture below. Who are they? What are they doing? Share your thoughts with your partner.

B What does a telephone operator do? Check the correct boxes.

ⓐ Handles phone calls to the hotel	☐	ⓑ Connects calls to guest rooms	☐
ⓒ Makes room reservations	☐	ⓓ Takes orders from guests	☐
ⓔ Delivers room service	☐	ⓕ Makes wakeup calls to guests	☐
ⓖ Gives information and directions	☐	ⓗ Deals with requests from guests at the front desk	☐

  Match each word or phrase with its correct definition.

1 put through	•	ⓐ to wait and not hang up the phone
2 stay on the line	•	ⓑ to state the letters of a word in order
3 engaged	•	ⓒ to be in a particular place
4 be located	•	ⓓ to connect someone to someone else on the telephone; to transfer
5 call back	•	ⓔ busy
6 step out	•	ⓕ to leave a place for a short amount of time
7 last name	•	ⓖ another term for a surname; a family name
8 spell	•	ⓗ to call again

Hotel Terminology Learn the following words and phrases used in the hotel industry.

hotel limousine   a hotel car driven by a hotel driver according to passengers' requests

house phone   a telephone mainly installed in a hotel lobby; a telephone one can use to call a hotel operator or guest rooms

operator   an employee who connects telephone calls to requested departments or guest rooms

PBX   private branch exchange; a telephone system that handles the internal and external calls of a hotel

switchboard   a place in a hotel where all the telephone calls are connected

wakeup call   a service which involves calling guests in their rooms at certain times to wake them up

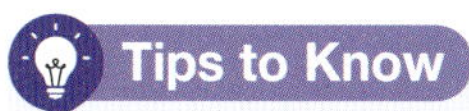
Tips to Know

Spelling Alphabet

A spelling alphabet, which is often called a radio alphabet or a telephone alphabet, is a set of words used to stand for the letters of the alphabet in oral communication. When speaking on the telephone, a person can find it useful to spell a word by using the spelling alphabet. For example, to spell PARK, you could say, "P for Papa, A for Alpha, R for Romeo, K for Kilo."

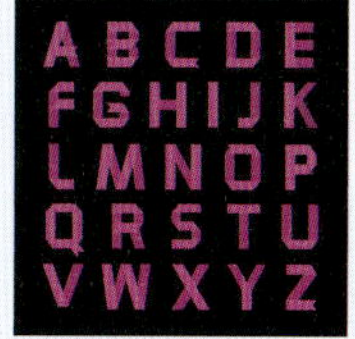

Alpha	Bravo	Charlie	Delta	Echo	Foxtrot	Golf	Hotel	India	Juliet	Kilo	Lima	Mike
November	Oscar	Papa	Quebec	Romeo	Sierra	Tango	Uniform	Victor	Whiskey	X-ray	Yankee	Zulu

A Giving information about transportation

🎧 01-01

Operator	Thank you for calling the Emerald Hotel. This is Linda speaking. How may I assist you?[1]
Caller	Hello. How can I get to your hotel from Incheon International Airport?
Operator	You can take a taxi, an airport limousine bus, or our hotel limousine. Which one would you prefer?
Caller	This is my first business trip to Korea, and I need to stop by the COEX Center before I go to the hotel.
Operator	Well, why don't you use our limousine service?[2] We can drop you off at the COEX Center and then take your luggage to the hotel.
Caller	That's wonderful! I'm definitely going to use the limousine service then.
Operator	You can reserve it when you make a room reservation. The limousine pickup service fee is 140,000 won, and it can be charged to your room. Do you need anything else before I transfer your call?
Caller	No, thank you.
Operator	Now, let me transfer you to the Reservation Department.[3] Have a wonderful day, sir!

Key & Alternative Expressions

1 How may I assist you?
= Can [May] I help you?
= How can I help you?
= What can I do for you?

2 Why don't you use our limousine service?
= I recommend that you use our limousine service.
= How about using our limousine service?
= May I suggest using our limousine service?

3 Let me transfer you to the Reservation Department.
= I will transfer you to the Reservation Department.
= Let me put you through to the Reservation Department.
= I will connect you to the Reservation Department.

Operator	Thank you for calling the Lunar Hotel. This is David speaking. How may I help you?
Caller	Hello. Does your hotel have a swimming pool?
Operator	We sure do, ma'am. It is located on the 5th floor inside the fitness club.
Caller	Excellent. How late is the swimming pool open?
Operator	It is open from 7 A.M. until 10 P.M.
Caller	Great! Thank you for the information.
Operator	My pleasure.

Say the following sentences in English.

1 Lunar 호텔에 전화해주셔서 감사합니다.

2 호텔에 수영장이 있나요?

3 수영장은 5층 피트니스 클럽 안에 있습니다.

4 수영장은 오전 7시부터 오후 10시까지 엽니다.

Operator	Good afternoon, Mr. Stewart. This is Gloria speaking. How may I help you?
Guest	I'd like to watch a movie in my room. How much is it?
Operator	It's 15,000 won to watch one movie and 20,000 won to watch movies all day.
Guest	Okay.
Operator	Is there anything else I can help you with?
Guest	No, thank you.

Say the following sentences in English.

1 무엇을 도와드릴까요?

2 영화 한 편을 시청하는 것은 15,000원이며 종일 시청하는 것은 20,000원입니다.

3 더 도와드릴 것 있습니까?

Operator	Good evening, Ms. Smith. May I help you?
Guest	Good evening. Where can I have breakfast tomorrow?
Operator	You can have breakfast at the cafe in the lobby, or you can order room service.
Guest	Thank you.
Operator	Can I help you with anything else today?
Guest	Yes, when is breakfast served?
Operator	The breakfast buffet is served from 5 A.M. to 10 A.M., and room service is available 24 hours a day.
Guest	That's good to know. I appreciate your help.
Operator	You're welcome, Ms. Smith.

Say the following sentences in English.

1 로비에 있는 카페에서 조식을 드실 수 있습니다.

2 조식 뷔페는 오전 5시부터 오전 10시까지 제공됩니다.

3 룸서비스는 하루 24시간 이용하실 수 있습니다.

Essential Expressions　Giving Information

1 Answering phone calls

Thank you for calling the OOO Hotel. This is OOO speaking. How may I assist you?

2 Connecting phone calls

Let me put you through

Let me transfer you　　}　+　to (department).

Let me connect you

3 Suggesting additional help (before ending the phone call)

Do you need anything else?

Do you need any other assistance?

Is there anything else I can help you with?

Can I help you with anything else today?

4 Expressions to respond to "Thank you" (general)

Causal	Polite
You're welcome. / That's all right.	I'm glad to be of service to you.
No problem. / No big deal!	I'm happy to be of service to you.
It's nothing. / Not at all.	I'm glad I could help you.
Sure. / Sure thing.	It's my pleasure to be of service to you.
No worries. / Don't mention it.	It was my pleasure to assist you.
You got it. / Anytime.	I'm happy to help.
No, no. Thank You.	

A Connecting a call to a guest's room

🎧 01-05

Operator	Good afternoon. Nova Hotel. This is Susana speaking. How may I assist you?
Caller	Hello. Would you put me through to Mr. Gilbert in room 1004?[1]
Operator	Of course, sir. Please stay on the line.[2] I will connect you.
	(A few seconds later…)
Operator	I'm sorry, but nobody is answering the phone. Can I take a message?[3]
Caller	Yes, please. Can you tell him that Harry Schultz phoned?
Operator	Certainly, sir. Could you spell your last name, please?[4]
Caller	Yes. That's S-C-H-U-L-T-Z. He's got my number.
Operator	That's S for Sam, C for Charlie, H for hotel, U for uniform, L for Love, T for Tom, and Z for Zebra?
Caller	You've got it!
Operator	Thank you, Mr. Shultz. I'll make sure Mr. Gilbert gets your message.
Caller	Thank you very much.
Operator	It was my pleasure.

Key & Alternative Expressions

1 Would you put me through to Mr. Gilbert in room 1004?

= Can you connect [transfer] me to Mr. Gilbert's room?

= Can I speak to Mr. Gilbert?

2 Please stay on the line.

= Hold the line, please. = Hold on (a moment), please. = Could you please hold? = Would you like to hold?

= Would you hold the line? = May I put you on hold?

3 Can I take a message?

= Can I give him a message?

= Would you like me to take a message?

= Would you like to leave a message?

= Do you want to leave a message?

cf. What's your number, please?

Does he have your number?

4 Could you spell your last name, please?

= How do you spell your last name?

= How is your last name spelled?

Agent: Sales & Marketing Agent

Operator	Good morning. Jack speaking. How can I assist you?
Caller	I'd like to speak to Mr. Lee in Sales & Marketing.
Operator	May I ask who is calling, please?
Caller	Yes, my name is Sarah White.
Operator	Certainly, Ms. White. One moment, please.
	(A few seconds later...)
Operator	I'm sorry, but the line is busy. Would you like to leave a message?
Caller	Can you try one more time?
Operator	Sure, ma'am. Let me try once again.
	(A few seconds later...)
Agent	Good morning. Michael speaking. How may I assist you?
Caller	May I speak to Mr. Lee, please?
Agent	I'm afraid Mr. Lee just stepped out of the office.
Caller	When do you expect him back?
Agent	I'm not sure, but he will probably be back by three. Shall I have him call you when he returns to the office?
Caller	No, that's all right. I'll call back later. Thank you.
Agent	My pleasure.

Say the following sentences in English.

1 누구신지 여쭤봐도 될까요?

2 죄송하지만, 지금 통화 중이십니다.

3 말씀 전해드릴까요?

4 죄송하지만 Lee 씨는 방금 사무실에서 나가셨습니다.

5 아마 3시까지는 돌아오실 겁니다.

6 사무실에 돌아오시면 전화 드리라고 할까요?

🎧 01-07 

Operator	Good evening. Tiffany speaking. What can I do for you?
Guest	Hello. Could you give me a wakeup call at six tomorrow morning?
Operator	Absolutely, Mr. Brown. We'll call you at 6 A.M. tomorrow. Good night, sir.
Guest	Thank you. Good night.
	(The next morning…)
Guest	Hello?
Operator	Good morning, Mr. Brown. This is your 6 A.M. wakeup call.
Guest	Thank you.
Operator	You're welcome, sir. Have a great day.

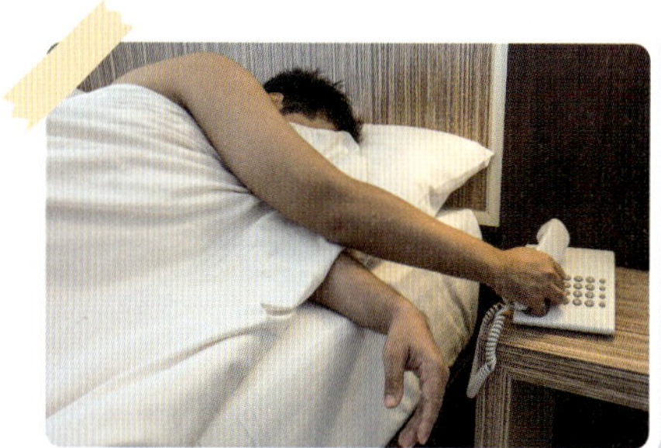

Say the following sentences in English.

1 안녕하세요. Tiffany입니다. 무엇을 도와드릴까요?

2 내일 아침 6시에 모닝콜 좀 해주시겠습니까?

3 좋은 아침입니다, Brown 씨. 오전 6시 모닝콜입니다.

4 좋은 하루 보내십시오.

D **Handling a wrong number**

🎧 01-08 

Operator	Good afternoon. Sunshine Hotel. This is Carl speaking. How may I assist you?
Caller	May I speak to Mr. James Chung in room 1105?
Operator	Just a moment, ma'am… I'm sorry, but Mr. Chung is not a guest at this hotel.
Caller	Oh, really? But he told me to call here.
Operator	I'm sorry, but there is no one here by that name. What number are you calling?
Caller	Isn't this the Sunset Hotel?
Operator	Oh, no, this is the Sunshine Hotel. I'm afraid you called the wrong hotel.

Say the following sentences in English.

1 Chung 씨는 이 호텔 고객이 아닙니다.

2 죄송하지만, 여기 그런 성함을 가진 고객은 없습니다.

3 몇 번으로 전화하셨습니까?

4 죄송하지만 다른 호텔에 거셨습니다.

1   Asking for the caller's name

May I ask who is calling, please?

Who's calling, please?

Where are you calling from?

cf. I didn't catch your name.

2   When failing to connect a call

I'm sorry, but the line is busy [engaged].

I'm sorry, but nobody is answering the phone.

I'm afraid he's on another line.

Would you like to leave a message?

Would you please hold the line?

Could you call back later?

3   Promising to deliver messages (messenger service)

I'll make sure he gets your message.

I'll have him call you back.

I'll ask him to call you as soon as possible.

I'll give him the message when he comes back.

I'll tell him that you called.

4   Delivering messages

There is a message for you from Mr. White. He asked you to call him back as soon as you returned.

5   Telephone problems

I can't hear you very well.

The line is very bad.

Could you speak up a little, please?

I'm sorry. I didn't catch that [your name]. Could you repeat that, please?

Exercises

A Choose the best response to each question or statement.

1 A: Would you like to leave a message?

B: ___________________________

 ⓐ Yes, please.

 ⓑ I can take a message.

 ⓒ It would be my pleasure.

2 A: May I speak to Mr. Kim in the Sales Department?

B: ___________________________

 ⓐ I'll have him call you back.

 ⓑ He just stepped out of the office.

 ⓒ How can I help you?

3 A: I'd like to reserve the limousine pickup service, please.

B: ___________________________

 ⓐ Thank you for calling.

 ⓑ Let me put you through to the Reservation Department.

 ⓒ I'll make sure he gets the message.

4 A: Does your hotel have a business center?

B: ___________________________

 ⓐ I'm glad to hear that.

 ⓑ Don't mention it.

 ⓒ Yes, we do.

B Match each sentence with the best reply.

1 Would you wake me up at 7 tomorrow morning? •

2 May I ask who is calling, please? •

3 Would you like to leave a message? •

4 What number are you calling? •

5 When do you expect him back? •

 • ⓐ Certainly, sir. We will call you at 7 A.M.

 • ⓑ Isn't this the Ocean Hotel?

 • ⓒ I think he will be back by noon.

 • ⓓ No, that's all right. I'll call back later.

 • ⓔ Yes, my name is Doris Bell.

C Complete the following conversation with the words in the box.

busy	hold	connect	assist	speaking

Operator Good morning. This is Lisa ¹___________. How may I ²___________ you?

Caller Hi. Can you ³___________ me to Mr. Shaw's room?

Operator Certainly, ma'am. I'll connect you… I'm sorry, but the line is ⁴___________.
Would you ⁵___________ the line?

Caller No problem.

Role-Playing

A Use the web page below to practice giving information about the hotel. Take turns being an operator and a caller with your partner.

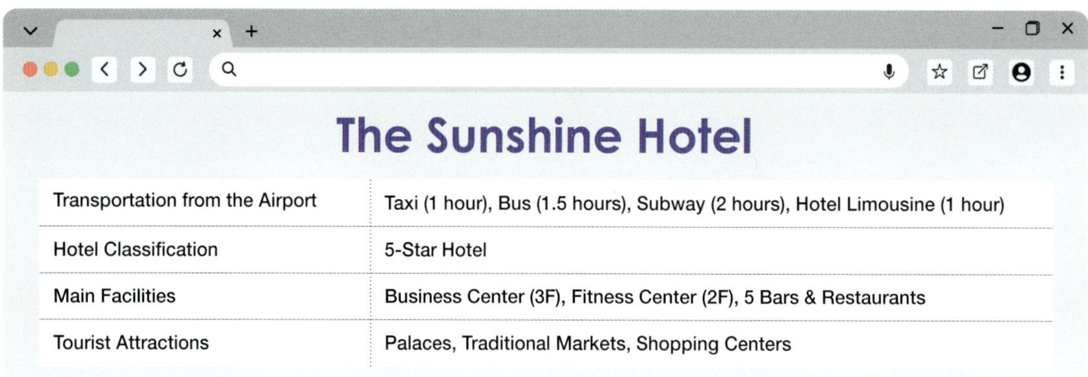

Transportation from the Airport	Taxi (1 hour), Bus (1.5 hours), Subway (2 hours), Hotel Limousine (1 hour)
Hotel Classification	5-Star Hotel
Main Facilities	Business Center (3F), Fitness Center (2F), 5 Bars & Restaurants
Tourist Attractions	Palaces, Traditional Markets, Shopping Centers

Example

Operator	Good morning. Sunshine Hotel. What can I help you with?
Caller	How can I get to the hotel from the airport?
Operator	You may take a taxi, a bus, a subway, or a hotel limousine.

B Practice handling the following situations. Take turns being an operator and a caller with your partner.

Situation 1

Connecting a call to a guest's room

Situation 2

Connecting a guest's call to an employee in a hotel department

Situation 3

Taking a request for a wakeup call

Situation 4

Handling a wrong number

Example

Operator	Good morning. Castle Hotel. How may I assist you?
Caller	Can I speak to Mr. Han in room 1030?
Operator	

Switchboard

The switchboard (PBX) at a hotel is the department which provides one of the most important services for guests. The switchboard employees are called operators, and they are ready to answer the phone around the clock. They not only connect all the phone calls at the hotel, but they also often greet hotel guests for the very first time when they call the hotel. Thus, it is important for them to make a good impression of the hotel on the guests. These operators work in the "back of the house," which is a hotel term that refers to a hidden office in a hotel that guests cannot see. They perform various tasks such as connecting phone calls, making wakeup calls, giving information and directions, and handling call charges.

Nowadays at some hotels, the switchboard functions as a one-call service or one-stop service department for the convenience of hotel guests. The operator takes orders from guests and distributes them to room service, the bell desk, housekeeping, and the front desk. Guests can therefore place all of their orders with operators at the switchboard, so there is no need to call different departments to make different orders.

Words & Phrases

around the clock   for 24 hours without stopping

convenience   the condition of being useful or suitable for a particular person

department   a section in an organization such as a government, a business, or a university

distribute   to give or deliver things to a number of people

function   to serve

greet   to welcome someone with polite words or actions

impression   the feeling you have about someone or something, usually after having seen or heard that person or thing

perform   to do a task

place an order   to order

- Taking Room Reservations
- Handling Requests After Reservations

02 Reservations

Warming Up

A Look at the pictures below. What are the differences between these three types of beds? Share your thoughts with your partner.

B Which information does a reservations agent ask a guest first when taking a reservation?

- ⓐ if the guest has stayed at the hotel before
- ⓑ the number of guests
- ⓒ the room type
- ⓓ the arrival date and number of nights the guest is staying
- ⓔ the name of the guest

arrange	extra	on behalf of	available	book	guarantee

1 _____________ phr as the representative of someone; instead of someone

2 _____________ v to reserve; to arrange to have something or to use it at a particular time

3 _____________ v to make plans for something to happen; to make it possible for someone to do something

4 _____________ adj requiring additional payment; additional

5 _____________ v to promise that something will definitely happen

6 _____________ adj able to be used or bought

Hotel Terminology Learn the following words and phrases used in the hotel industry.

cancelation charge a penalty for canceling a reservation

cancelation policy a set of plans about what to do when guests cancel their reservations

confirmation number a reservation number

ETA estimated time of arrival

executive floor a special floor in a hotel with enhanced service which is often designated for business travelers

extra bed a rollaway bed that can be temporarily set up in a hotel room

full house a situation in which every room is occupied

service charge a gratuity (usually 10% of the room rate or food & beverage charge)

triple room a room designed for three people to stay together, mostly preferred by families

Tips to Know

Types of Hotel Rooms

single a room assigned to one person (may have one bed)
double a room assigned to two people (may have one or more beds)
triple a room assigned to three people (may have two or more beds)
suite a parlor or living room connected to one or more bedrooms
connecting room a room connected to another one with a door opening between them (a connecting door)
adjoining rooms rooms with a common wall but no connecting door
adjacent rooms rooms close to each other, such as across the halls

A   Taking reservations

🎧 02-01

Agent: Reservations Agent

Agent	Imperial Hotel reservations. Sandra speaking. How may I assist you?
Caller	Hi. I'd like to reserve a room, please.
Agent	What day will you be arriving, sir?[1]
Caller	On May 23.
Agent	How long will you be staying with us?[2]
Caller	I will be staying for three nights. Do you have any rooms available?[3]
Agent	Let me check… Yes, we have a deluxe room available for those days. We can offer you a deluxe room for $250 a night plus tax and service charges. Will that be suitable?
Caller	Is breakfast included?
Agent	No, breakfast is extra. You can enjoy it at the restaurant and charge the bill to your room.
Caller	That's fine. I'll take it.
Agent	May I have your name and phone number? Have you stayed with us before?
Caller	My name is Colin Sellers. This is my first visit. And my number is (202) 555-0160.
Agent	Very good, Mr. Sellers. Your room has been reserved from May 23 to 26, and your confirmation number is 17502. Thank you for calling. We look forward to seeing you then.

Key & Alternative Expressions

1 What day will you be arriving, sir?
= When are you going to check in?
= When do you plan to check in?
= When would you like to stay with us?
= What is the date of your arrival?
= On what day will you be arriving?

2 How long will you be staying with us?
= How many nights will you be staying?
= How many nights do you wish to stay?

3 Do you have any rooms available?
= Do you have any vacancies?
= Are there any rooms available?

 Explaining a cancelation policy

Agent: Reservations Agent

Caller	Hello? Can I speak to someone in Reservations?
Agent	This is the reservation desk. Brandon speaking. How may I help you?
Caller	I'd like to book a room for two for this Saturday night. Are there any rooms available?
Agent	Certainly, ma'am. How many nights will you be staying?
Caller	I'll just be there for one night.
Agent	Okay, ma'am. We have a double room available for this Saturday. The rate is $250 per night, including tax and service charges. Would you like to book it?
Caller	Yes, please. Oh, by the way, what is your cancelation policy?
Agent	Should you need to cancel your reservation, please let us know 24 hours prior to your scheduled arrival time.

Say the following sentences in English.

1 예약 가능한 방이 있습니까?

2 며칠 투숙하실 예정입니까?

3 요금은 1박에 250달러이며, 세금과 봉사료를 포함한 가격입니다.

4 (예약) 취소 규정이 어떻게 되나요?

 Putting a customer on the waiting list

Agent: Reservations Agent

Agent	Holiday Hotel reservations. Anna speaking. How may I help you?
Caller	Hello. I'm trying to reserve a room for this weekend.
Agent	I'm awfully sorry, but we have no rooms available for this weekend. Shall I give you the number of another hotel nearby?
Caller	Well, can you just put me on the waiting list?
Agent	Of course, sir. May I have your name and contact number? If there is a cancelation, I'll let you know.

Say the following sentences in English.

1 이번 주말에 객실을 예약하고 싶은데요.

2 정말 죄송합니다만, 이번 주말에는 예약 가능한 객실이 없습니다.

3 근처에 있는 다른 호텔 전화번호를 안내해드릴까요?

4 그냥 저를 대기자 명단에 넣어주실 수 있나요?

Agent: Reservations Agent

Caller	Hello. I'll be arriving on the 15th of July and will be staying until the 17th. Do you have any rooms available on the executive floor?
Agent	Yes, sir. We have rooms on the executive floor, and they include the full range of executive services.
Caller	Excellent. Can I make a reservation for that?
Agent	Certainly. May I have your name, please?
Caller	I'm Joseph Lee from New York. I'm a gold-level member of your hotel.
Agent	It's nice to have you back, Mr. Lee. Would you like to use the same credit card on file? It's a MasterCard.
Caller	No, I want to use my Visa card.
Agent	Could you give me the credit card number to guarantee the reservation?
Caller	Sure. The number is 4485 5320 8157 6223, and the expiration date is December 25, 2025.
Agent	All right, sir. You're all set. Your confirmation number is 17503. Is there anything else I can help you with?
Caller	Yes. Do you have limousine service from the airport?
Agent	We sure do. Please let me know your flight number and your time of arrival. I'll arrange it for you.

Say the following sentences in English.

1 비지니스전용층에 예약 가능한 방이 있나요?

2 다시 모시게 되어 반갑습니다, Lee 씨.

3 저희 기록에 있는 신용카드를 사용하시겠습니까?

4 예약을 보장하기 위해 신용카드 번호를 말씀해주시겠습니까?

5 다 되셨습니다.

6 비행기 편명과 도착 예정 시각을 말씀해주십시오.

Agent	Good morning. Hillside Hotel reservations. Aaron speaking. How may I assist you?
Caller	I would like to reserve a room for my family vacation. Can you recommend a room for me?
Agent	Certainly. When are you going to check in, ma'am?
Caller	On March 10 for 3 nights.
Agent	How many are you in your family?
Caller	We're a family of four. I'm traveling with my husband and 2 children.
Agent	How old are your kids?
Caller	They are 10 and 8 years old.
Agent	Well… I recommend that you book connecting rooms or a triple room with an extra bed in it. Which one do you prefer?
Caller	A triple room with an extra bed will be fine. I would like to be in the same room as my kids. What is the room rate?
Agent	It's $230 a night, and there is a $30 charge for an extra bed.
Caller	Can I have a room with an ocean view?
Agent	I'm afraid that I can't guarantee a room with that view. However, I'll make a special request to the front desk.

> **Say the following sentences in English.**

1 가족이 몇 분이십니까?

2 자녀분들 나이가 어떻게 되십니까?

3 침대를 추가하셔서 30달러의 요금이 있습니다.

Essential Expressions   Taking Room Reservations

1 **Asking a guest the number of people to stay**

How many people will be staying in the room?

How many are in your party [group / family]?

How many people are in your party [group / family]?

How large is your party [group / family]?

How many people is the reservation for?

How many adults will be in the room?

2 **Saying that a hotel has a full house**

We are fully booked for that period.

We are completely booked for Christmas this year.

We have no rooms available for this weekend.

We don't have any rooms available until the 18th of this month.

All our single rooms are reserved. The only room we have available is a twin room.

A Confirming reservations

🎧 02-06

Agent: Reservations Agent

Agent	Good afternoon. Jade Hotel. Amy speaking. How may I assist you?
Caller	I'd like to confirm my reservation, please. Can you help me with that?
Agent	Absolutely, sir. Could you tell me your name and reservation number?
Caller	My name is Hugo Hunter, but I'm afraid I don't remember my reservation number.
Agent	That's all right. Let me check on that...[1] Mr. Hunter, you reserved a double room for 2 nights starting on August 15.[2] You requested a nonsmoking room on a high floor.
Caller	That's right. Can you send me a confirmation email?
Agent	Certainly, sir. I'll send it to you right away.
Caller	Thank you.
Agent	My pleasure, sir.[3]

Key & Alternative Expressions

1 Let me check on that.
= Let me check your reservation details.
= Let me check if we have your reservation (on the system).
= Let me look you up on the system.

2 You reserved a double room for 2 nights starting on August 15.
= You will be staying in a double room for 2 nights starting on August 15.
= We have a reservation for you from August 15 to August 17.
= You are going to stay with us for 2 nights starting on August 15.

3 My pleasure, sir.
= It was my pleasure, sir.
= You're welcome, sir.
= I'm happy to help, sir.
= No problem, sir.

Agent: Reservations Agent

Caller	Hello. My name is Roy McDonald. I'd like to change my reservation, please.
Agent	Certainly, Mr. McDonald. Do you have the reservation number?
Caller	I'm afraid not.
Agent	That's all right. Let me check on that. One moment, please… You have a reservation for a deluxe twin room for 3 nights starting on May 23.
Caller	That's correct. But can I change the arrival date to May 11?
Agent	Just a moment… Okay, sir. I've changed that for you. Your reservation number is 17110.
Caller	I appreciate it.
Agent	You're welcome, sir. We will see you on May 11.

Say the following sentences in English.

1 예약을 변경하고 싶습니다.

2 확인해보겠습니다.

3 디럭스 트윈룸으로 5월 23일부터 3박 예약되어 있으시네요.

4 그렇게 변경해드렸습니다.

C Canceling reservations

🎧 02-08

Agent: Reservations Agent

Caller	I'd like to cancel a reservation, please.
Agent	May I have your name and reservation number?
Caller	I'm calling on behalf of Mr. David Johns. The reservation number is 17157. It is a reservation for June 15.
Agent	Excuse me, but may I ask who is calling?
Caller	I'm Julia Green, Mr. Johns's secretary.
Agent	Sure. May I ask why he is canceling? And can I have your phone number?
Caller	No problem. His business trip to Korea has been canceled, and my number is (305) 321-6542.
Agent	Thank you. I've canceled his reservation. We hope to serve him the next time he is in town.

Say the following sentences in English.

1 예약을 취소하려고 합니다.

2 David Johns 씨 대신 전화 드렸습니다.

3 실례지만, 전화 주신 분은 어떻게 되십니까?

4 그분의 예약을 취소해드렸습니다.

Essential Expressions — Handling Requests After Reservations

1 Expressing strong agreement
Absolutely. / Certainly.
Of course. / Very good.

2 Confirming reservations, changes, and cancelations
Your reservation has been made [changed / canceled].
I've made [changed / canceled] your reservation for you.

3 Saying goodbye to a guest who just canceled a reservation
We look forward to serving you next time.
We hope to serve you next time.
Please call again the next time you visit.
Please remember us in the future.

A Choose the best response to each question or statement.

1 A: Do you have any rooms available?

B: _______________________

   ⓐ Yes, we have 350 rooms in total.

   ⓑ I'd like to reserve a room.

   ⓒ I'm afraid we have a full house today.

2 A: We're a family of three. Can you recommend a room for us?

B: _______________________

   ⓐ How about staying in a triple room?

   ⓑ The single rooms are all booked.

   ⓒ You can come in with your children.

3 A: What is the room rate?

B: _______________________

   ⓐ I can offer you a room for $200 a night.

   ⓑ Tax and service charges are included.

   ⓒ You can get a group discount.

4 A: Do you want me to give you the number of another hotel nearby?

B: _______________________

   ⓐ Can I have your name?

   ⓑ Yes, that would be great.

   ⓒ I'm very sorry, sir.

B Match each sentence with the best reply.

1 Is breakfast included?

2 How many nights will you be staying?

3 Have you stayed with us before?

4 What is your cancelation policy?

5 Can you put me on the waiting list?

ⓐ I'm going to stay for two nights.

ⓑ Please let us know 24 hours prior to your scheduled arrival time.

ⓒ No, this is my first trip to Korea.

ⓓ Certainly. If there is a cancelation, I'll let you know.

ⓔ I'm afraid breakfast is extra.

C Complete the following conversation with the words in the box.

including	staying	arriving	offer	vacancies

Agent	Good morning. White Hotel. Miranda speaking. May I help you?
Caller	Do you have any ¹ _______________?
Agent	What day will you be ² _______________?
Caller	On May 5, and I'll be ³ _______________ for a week.
Agent	I can ⁴ _______________ you a deluxe room for $250 per night, ⁵ _______________ tax and service charges.
Caller	Very good. I will take it.

Role-Playing

A Use the room tariffs below to practice taking room reservations on the phone. Take turns being a reservations agent and a caller with your partner.

Sunshine Hotel Room Tariffs

• Standard Rooms
Deluxe	$200
Grand Deluxe	$250

• Executive Rooms
Deluxe	$300
Grand Deluxe	$350

• Suites
Superior	$500
Royal	$800
Presidential	$1,000

The above rates are subject to a 10% service charge and a 10% government tax.

Example

Agent Thank you for calling. Sunshine Hotel reservations. Jane speaking. How may I assist you?

Caller Do you have any rooms available?

Agent What type of room would you like?

Caller _______________

B Use the confirmation mail below to practice confirming and canceling reservations. Take turns being a reservations agent and a caller with your partner.

Reservation Confirmation

Dear Mr. Smith,

Thank you for choosing to stay with us at the Mirage Hotel. We are pleased to confirm your reservation as follows:

Confirmation Number:	237029
Guest Name:	Mr. Smith, John
Arrival Date:	05/15/2021
Departure Date:	05/18/2021
Number of Guests:	2
Accommodations:	Royal Suite
Rate per Night:	$800.00
Check-in Time:	3:00 P.M.
Checkout Time:	12:00 P.M.

Rates are subject to applicable state and local taxes. If you need to cancel this reservation, the Mirage Hotel requires notification by 3:00 P.M. the day before your arrival to avoid a charge for one night's room rate.

Should you have any requests, please feel free to call us at 1-800-800-8000 or email us at reservations@mirage.com.

We look forward to the pleasure of having you as our guest at the Mirage Hotel.

Sincerely,

Sandra Jones
Reservations Department

Example

Agent Thank you for calling. Reservations. Sandra speaking. How may I assist you?

Caller I'd like to confirm/cancel my reservation, please.

Agent _______________

Reservations

Reservations can be made in various ways, such as by telephone, travel agent, fax, letter, the Internet, and email, and there are also walk-in guests. Nowadays, one can easily book a hotel room online without having to speak a word. However, there are still many people who prefer talking to a person when they reserve a room. These potential guests call hotels and talk to the agents in the Reservation Department. Reservations agents mainly work in hidden offices like operators do. Guests call them to make inquiries, and then they decide whether to stay or not. That is why the reservation agents must have excellent communication skills and phone etiquette when speaking with guests.

When receiving a phone call, the reservations agent should first ask when the guest will arrive at the hotel and how long he or she will stay there. If there are any available rooms, the agent will ask about the type of room the guest wants. The agent will also ask the guest's name and his or her credit card number to guarantee the reservation and then find out if there are any other special requests.

During the peak season, reservations agents sometimes overbook rooms in case there are any cancelations or no-shows. By doing that, the hotel tries to have a full house to maximize its profits. However, overbooking can sometimes mean the hotel has to turn away some of its guests and send them to other hotels. Therefore, overbooking should be done carefully.

📝 Words & Phrases

etiquette   rules indicating the proper and polite way to behave

guarantee   to promise that something will definitely happen

have a full house   to have no vacancy; to be fully booked

inquiry   a question which you ask in order to get some information

no-show   a person who is expected to be somewhere but does not show up

overbook   to accept reservations in excess of the available space

turn away   to send someone to another hotel due to overbooking

walk-in guest   a guest who arrives with no reservation

UNIT 03 Door & Bell Desk

A Look at the two pictures below. Who are they? What do they do? Share your thoughts with your partner.

B Choose the picture that shows something a bellman does NOT do.

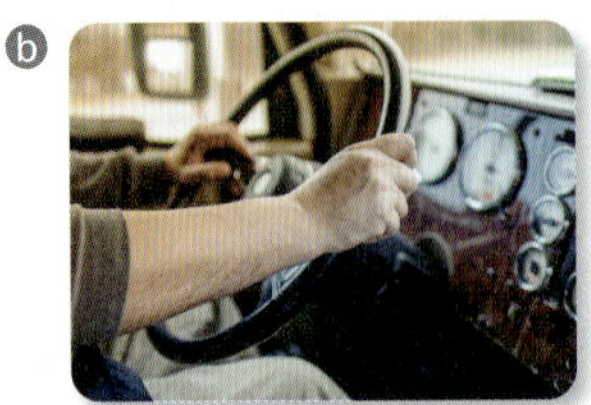

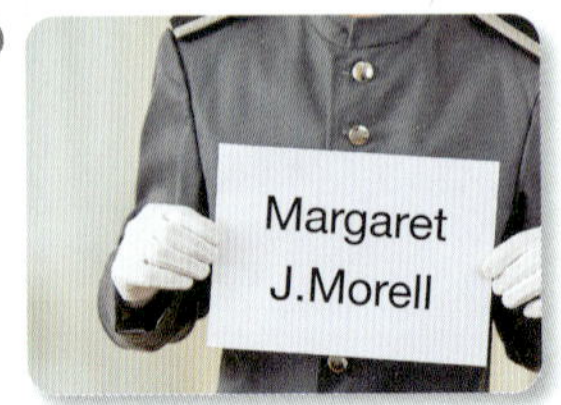

 Write the correct word or phrase for each definition.

inconvenience	revolving door	shelf	escort	spacious	unload

1 ______________ [n] a set of doors that you go through by pushing them around in a circle

2 ______________ [n] something causing problems or difficulties

3 ______________ [v] to take goods from a car

4 ______________ [v] to take someone somewhere

5 ______________ [adj] large in size or area; roomy; huge; large

6 ______________ [n] a flat piece of wood, glass, or metal used to keep things on

 Learn the following words and phrases used in the hotel industry.

baggage claim tag   a ticket given to hotel guests to prove that the baggage is theirs

baggage down service   a service that brings guests' baggage down to the lobby; a baggage collection service

bellman   a man who carries guests' bags in a hotel; a bellhop; a bellboy

checkroom   a room in a hotel where guests can leave their coats and other personal things; a cloakroom

doorman   a man who stands by the door of a hotel and lets people in or out

minibar   a small fridge in a hotel room, with beverages and light snacks inside

paging service   a service in which a bellman calls the names of guests to find them for other guests in a public place or to take messages from guests to other guests

safe   a strong metal box with a lock where people can keep their money or valuable things in a guest room

valet parking   a service in which guests' cars are parked for them

 **Tips to Know**

Doorman vs. Bellman

What's the difference between a doorman and a bellman? The major difference is the working area on the hotel premises. A doorman works in the area outside the hotel lobby and handles all the guest services that take place outdoors. On the other hand, a bellman works in the hotel lobby and visits almost all of the indoor places on the hotel premises, including the guest rooms.

A Welcoming a guest

🎧 03-01 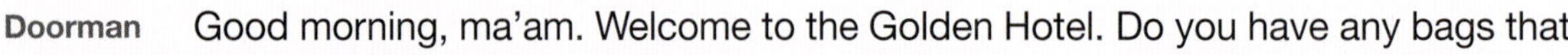

Doorman	Good morning, ma'am. Welcome to the Golden Hotel. Do you have any bags that I can help you with?
Guest	Yes. I have a couple of bags in the trunk.
Doorman	Let me unload them, ma'am. Our bellman will take care of your baggage afterward.
Guest	That's nice. Where do I register?[1]
Doorman	The front desk is over there to your left. Please watch out for the revolving door.
Guest	Thank you.
Doorman	It's my pleasure. Have a good stay with us.[2]

B Helping a guest with a taxi

🎧 03-02 

Doorman	Good afternoon, ma'am. Would you like a taxi?[3]
Guest	Yes, please. I'm going to Namdaemun Market.
Doorman	Please have a seat in the lobby, ma'am. I'll let you know when one is ready for you.
Guest	Thank you. How long does it take to get there from here?
Doorman	Well, it normally takes about 10 minutes[4], but it may take longer depending on traffic.

Key & Alternative Expressions

1 Where do I register?
= Where is the front desk? = Where can I check in? = Where is the reception desk?

2 Have a good stay with us.
= Please enjoy your stay (with us). = Have a nice stay (with us). = I wish you a wonderful stay with us.

3 Would you like a taxi?
= Do you need a taxi [cab]? = Shall I call a taxi [cab] for you? = Do you want me to catch [grab] a taxi [cab] for you?

4 It normally takes about 10 minutes.
= It takes 10 minutes on foot [by taxi / by subway / by bus] from here.
= It is 10 minutes away from here.
= It is a 10-minute walk [drive] from here.

C Valet parking services I

🎧 03-03

Doorman	Good afternoon, ma'am.
	Can I help you?
Guest	Where should I park my car?
Doorman	You can use our valet parking service.
	Just leave your car here.
	I will have someone take care of everything.
Guest	Great. Thank you.
Doorman	You're welcome, ma'am.

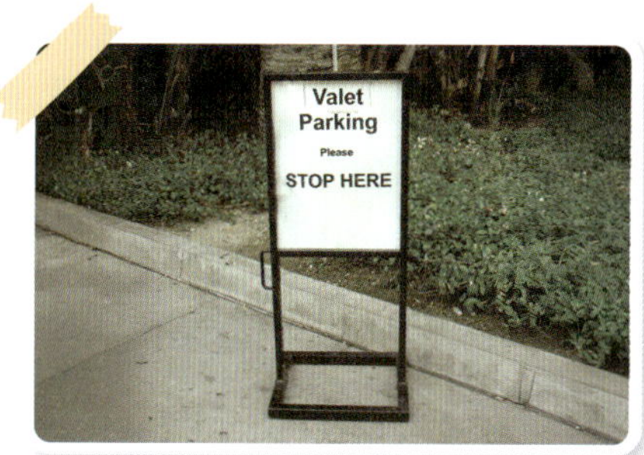

Say the following sentences in English.

1 차를 어디에다 대야 하나요?

2 그냥 여기에 차를 두고 가십시오.

3 담당 직원에게 처리하라고 하겠습니다.

D Valet parking services II

🎧 03-04

Doorman	Good evening, ma'am.
	What can I do for you?
Guest	Could you get my car, please?
Doorman	Of course, ma'am. What's the plate number?
Guest	The number is 4577. It's a black car.
Doorman	I'll bring it immediately. Just one moment, please.
Guest	Thank you very much.
Doorman	My pleasure.

Say the following sentences in English.

1 제 차를 가져다주시겠습니까?

2 차량 번호가 어떻게 되십니까?

3 고객님의 차를 즉시 가져오겠습니다.

Doorman	Good morning, ma'am. Are you leaving now?
Guest	Yes, I am.
Doorman	Did you enjoy your stay with us?
Guest	Yes, I had a wonderful time.
	I'll definitely come back here again!
Doorman	I'm pleased to hear that. Do you need a taxi?
Guest	Yes, I do.
	(Doorman waves to a taxi standing by…)
Doorman	Here comes a taxi. I'll put your luggage in the trunk.
Guest	Thank you so much.
Doorman	Enjoy your trip, ma'am.

Say the following sentences in English.

1 지금 가십니까?

2 저희 호텔에서 편안하게 쉬셨습니까?

3 그 말씀을 들으니 기쁩니다.

4 택시가 필요하십니까?

5 택시가 오네요.

6 제가 짐을 트렁크에 실어드리겠습니다.

Essential Expressions   Doorman Service

1 Greeting a guest in front of the door

Good morning [afternoon / evening], ma'am [sir].
Welcome to the Golden Hotel.

Do you have any bags that I can help you with?
Do you have any luggage with you?
May I help you with your luggage?

2 Saying that a bellman will take care of a guest's baggage

Our bellman will take care of your baggage.
A bellman will take your bags to your room.
Our bellboy will assist you with your luggage.

3 Asking a guest to be careful

Please watch out for the revolving door.
Watch your step. The road is slippery.
Mind your head, please.

4 Suggesting a guest to wait inside

Please have a seat in the lobby. I'll let you know when a taxi is ready.
Would you like to wait inside, ma'am? I will call you when a cab arrives.

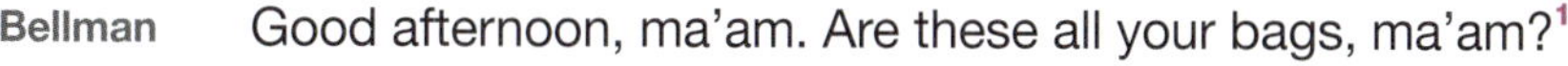

A Taking a guest to his or her room

🎧 03-06

Bellman	Good afternoon, ma'am. Are these all your bags, ma'am?[1]
Guest	Yes, these are all of them.
Bellman	May I have your keycard?
Guest	Here it is.
Bellman	Thank you. Let me escort you to your room, ma'am. This way, please…[2] Please take the elevator. After you, ma'am.[3]
Guest	Thanks.
Bellman	Your room is on the 16th floor… Here we are. After you, ma'am.
	(They get out of the elevator.)
Bellman	Your room is on the right side. This way, please.
	(They arrive at the door.)
Bellman	This is your room. Please go in. Where shall I put your bags?
Guest	Over there is fine. Thanks. This room is nicer and more spacious than I expected. I love the view overlooking downtown.
Bellman	I'm glad you like the room, ma'am.

Key & Alternative Expressions

1 Are these all your bags, ma'am?
= Is there any other baggage?
= Do you have any other bags?
= How many pieces of baggage do you have?

2 This way, please.
= Please come with me.
= Please follow me.
= Step this way, please.

3 After you, ma'am.
= Please go first.

B Showing a guest his or her room

∩ 03-07

Bell Captain Let me show you your room, sir. Here is the light switch for the bathroom. The temperature controller is right here. A safe is in the built-in closet right there. Your minibar is in the cabinet over there, and the price list is on the shelf. You'll get charged for what you use when you check out. There are two bottles of complimentary mineral water on the shelf.

Guest You've been very helpful. This is for you.

Bell Captain I'm sorry, sir. Our hotel has a no-tipping policy. A service charge will be added to your final bill.

Guest Oh, really? Thank you.

Bell Captain The pleasure is all mine, sir. Enjoy your stay. If you need any other assistance, please call the bell desk at any time.

Say the following sentences in English.

1 제가 객실을 보여드리겠습니다.

2 사용하신 것은 체크아웃하실 때 청구될 겁니다.

3 무료 생수 두 병이 선반 위에 있습니다.

4 저희 호텔은 팁을 받지 않습니다.

5 봉사료는 최종 계산서에 합산될 겁니다.

C Baggage down service

∩ 03-08

Bell Captain Good morning. This is the bell desk. Peter speaking. How may I assist you?

Guest Good morning. Can you send a bellman to my room? I'm checking out in 10 minutes.

Bell Captain No problem, ma'am. May I have your name and room number?

Guest I'm Clara Hansen in room 1021.

Bell Captain Thank you, Ms. Hansen. How many bags do you have?

Guest I have two suitcases and one carry-on bag.

Bell Captain I see. I will send someone up immediately.

Say the following sentences in English.

1 제 방으로 벨맨을 보내주시겠습니까?

2 저는 10분 후에 체크아웃할 예정입니다.

3 가방이 몇 개나 되십니까?

4 여행용 가방 2개와 휴대용 가방 1개가 있습니다.

5 지금 바로 직원을 올려보내겠습니다.

D Holding baggage

🎧 03-09

Bellman Good morning, ma'am. How may I help you?

Guest Hi. Can my husband and I leave our bags at the hotel? We just checked out of our room, but we would like to go downtown to look around before leaving for the airport.

Bellman Sure. Let me store your luggage in our checkroom until you come back. Can I have your name and room number?

Guest I'm Shirley Carson, and I was in room 1004.

Bellman I see, Mrs. Carson. Are these your only bags?

Guest Yes. These three suitcases.

Bellman All right. Here is your baggage claim tag. Please keep this until you pick up your bags. Have a great time.

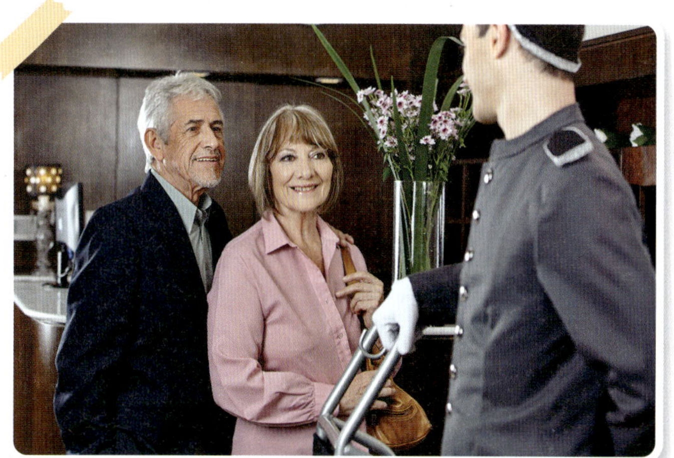

Say the following sentences in English.

1 저와 남편 가방을 호텔에 두고 가도 되나요?

2 돌아오실 때까지 짐을 보관소에 보관해드리겠습니다.

3 성함과 객실 번호를 알 수 있을까요?

4 이 가방들이 전부입니까?

5 수하물보관증 여기 있습니다.

Teacher's note 시간 표현에 쓰이는 전치사

전치사	의미	예문
in	• ~후에, ~뒤에, ~이 지나서 (특정 시간이 지난 시점) • 언급한 시간이 다 경과한 후/경계선 포함 가능	I'll be there in 1 hour. (1시간 후에 도착할 것이다.) I will finish the work in 3 days. (3일 후에 이 일을 끝낼 것이다.)
	• (일정시간) 만에	Today is the hottest day in 30 years. (오늘은 30년 만에 가장 더운 날입니다.) He finished the homework in 2 hours. (그는 숙제를 2시간 만에 끝냈어.)
within	• ~이내에, ~안에 (특정기간 이내) • 언급한 시간이 지나가기 전/경계선 포함	I will be there within 3 days. 3일 이내에 도착할 것이다. (3일째 되는 날까지 포함) I will finish the work within 3 days. 3일 이내에 (3일째 되는 날까지) 이 일을 끝낼 것이다.
after	• ~후에, ~지나서 (특정시간 이후) • 언급한 시간 지난 후, 그 후로 계속되는 시간을 포함 (언제가 될지 모름)	I will be there after 1 hour. (1시간 후에 도착할 것이다.) I will finish the work after 3 days. (3일 지난 후에 이 일을 끝낼 것이다)

Bell Captain	Good afternoon. This is the bell desk. Alan speaking. Can I help you?
Guest	Yes, I'm Rose Baker in room 528. I've been waiting for my bags to be sent up for almost 30 minutes!
Bell Captain	I'm terribly sorry for the delay, Ms. Baker. Do you have a baggage tag number?
Guest	Yes. It's 0132.
Bell Captain	I'll check on that right away and get back to you, ma'am. (A few minutes later…)
Bell Captain	Hello. This is the bell captain. Alan speaking. Ms. Baker, your bags are on the way now. I'm very sorry for the inconvenience.

Say the following sentences in English.

1 거의 30분째 가방이 올라오기를 기다리고 있다고요!

2 지연이 되어 대단히 죄송합니다, Baker 씨.

3 제가 바로 확인해보고 다시 전화 드리겠습니다.

4 고객님 가방이 지금 올라가는 중입니다.

5 불편을 끼쳐드려 정말 죄송합니다.

Essential Expressions   **Bellman Service**

1 Asking guests where to put their bags

Where shall I put your bags?

Shall I put your bags over there?

I will put your bags over here.

2 Promising further assistance

If you need any other assistance, please call the bell desk at any time.

If you need anything, please feel free to contact us.

If you need any help, please dial 0.

3 Checking in baggage

Let me store your luggage in our checkroom until you come back.

We can keep your bags for you.

You can check your luggage at the bell desk.

We will hold your baggage until you come for it.

4 Apologizing politely

I'm very [terribly / extremely / awfully] sorry for the inconvenience.

I apologize for the inconvenience.

Please accept our sincere apology.

A Choose the best response to each question.

1 Who works outside the hotel premises?
   ⓐ a bell captain
   ⓑ a cashier
   ⓒ a doorman

2 Where can guests store their bags after they check out?
   ⓐ at the front desk
   ⓑ in the checkroom
   ⓒ in their rooms

3 Which is one of the responsibilities of the bellman?
   ⓐ valet parking
   ⓑ showing guests their rooms
   ⓒ delivering food

4 Who is the first employee a guest will meet after arriving at a hotel?
   ⓐ a bellman
   ⓑ a receptionist
   ⓒ a doorman

B Match each sentence with the best reply.

1 Where do I register?

2 Can you call a taxi for me?

3 Could you get my car?

4 Where shall I put your bags, ma'am?

5 I've been waiting for my bags for about 30 minutes!

ⓐ I'm very sorry for the inconvenience.

ⓑ The front desk is right over there.

ⓒ No problem, sir. What's the plate number?

ⓓ Over there, please.

ⓔ Absolutely. Please have a seat in the lobby while you wait.

C Complete the following conversation with the words in the box.

get	after	complimentary	charged	way

Bellman Let me escort you to your room, ma'am. This [1]___________, please… Please take the elevator. [2]___________ you, ma'am… This is your room. Please [3]___________ in. Where shall I put your bags?

Guest Over there is fine. Thanks.

Bellman There is a minibar in the cabinet.

Guest Are the items in it [4]___________?

Bellman I'm afraid not. You'll get [5]___________ for what you use when you check out. Only the two bottles of mineral water outside the minibar are free daily.

A Practice welcoming and helping a guest. Take turns being a doorman and a guest with your partner.

Example

Doorman   Good morning, ma'am. Welcome to the Cosmos Hotel.

Guest   Can you help with my baggage in the trunk?

Doorman   ....

B Practice escorting a guest to his room and helping him with his baggage. Take turns being a bellman and a guest.

Example

Bellman   Good afternoon, sir. May I have your room key?

Guest   Here it is.

Bellman   ....

Door and Bell Desks

The door desk is located outside the hotel's main entrance. It is the department whose workers greet guests first and see them off last. When a guest's car arrives, a doorman  opens the car door and says hello to the guest with a warm smile. Doormen are in charge of the parking area, so they provide valet parking service themselves, and they sometimes call taxis for hotel guests.

The bell desk is located in the lobby near the concierge desk or main entrance. When a guest arrives, a bellman helps the guests with his or her baggage and carries it to the front desk. Then, he waits until the guest finishes the check-in process.

Once the guest gets a room key, the bellman takes the guest to his or her room and explains what is in the room. When the guest checks out, the bellman takes the guest's baggage down to the lobby. This is not the only job bellmen do though. They deliver messages, mail, and packages to guests in their rooms and page guests as well. When guests don't answer wakeup calls, bellmen sometimes wake up the guests in person by knocking on their doors or even going into their rooms. A full-service hotel can have the bell desk open for 24 hours like the front desk.

As doormen and bellmen often give the first and last impressions of the hotel for guests, good language skills along with a helpful and friendly attitude are required for these positions.

Words & Phrases

concierge an employee who helps guests with information about the area where the hotel is, including transportation, restaurants, and tours

main entrance the main door

package a box that is sent by mail

see off to take someone to a point of departure to say goodbye

UNIT

04 Front Desk I (Reception)

A Look at the picture below. Where in a hotel is this place? What kinds of activities can take place here? Share your thoughts with your partner.

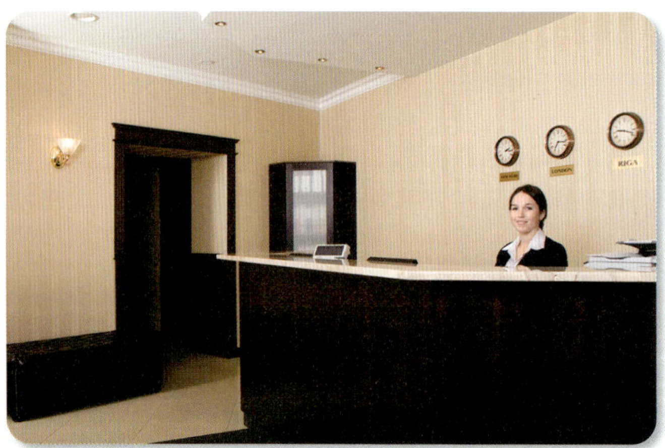

B Which item is NOT necessary for check-in?

ⓐ

ⓑ

ⓒ

ⓓ

  Write the correct word or phrase for each definition.

extend	imprint	set	inventory	closet	lock out	fill out	get through

1 _______________ **phr** to write all the necessary information on a document

2 _______________ **phr** to prevent someone from entering by locking a door

3 _______________ **n** a mark left by an object when it is printed or pressed onto something

4 _______________ **v** to make something last longer

5 _______________ **phr** to reach; to succeed in making contact

6 _______________ **adj** ready; prepared

7 _______________ **n** a list of all the things that are available

8 _______________ **n** a small room with a door used to keep things in; a wardrobe

Hotel Terminology Learn the following words and phrases used in the hotel industry.

adjoining room a room next to another with a common wall between them but without a connecting door

courtesy shuttle bus a free shuttle bus for a hotel's guests

OTA online travel agency

PMS property management system

receptionist an employee who helps guests who call or enter a hotel

registration the process of checking guests into a hotel by recording necessary information about them in a hotel system

room assignment the process of giving a guest a certain room

shift a particular period of work time during the day or night

walk-in guest a guest with no reservation; a walk-in

 **Tips to Know**

How to Calculate a Hotel Room Rate

Most of the hotels in Korea have a no-tipping policy. Instead, a service charge is included in the room rate. The rate is subject to a 10% service charge, and a 10% government tax is applied to the sum again. This means that you have to pay an extra 21% on your room rate. Let's put it this way. If the room rate is $100 per night, the service charge will be $10, and that will bring the total to $110. Thus, the government tax will be $11. So the total amount of money you have to pay for one night is $121 ($110 + $11).

A Check-in process I

04-01

Receptionist	Welcome to the Imperial. How may I help you?
Guest	Hi. I would like to check in, please.[1]
Receptionist	Do you have a reservation?[2]
Guest	Yes, I made a reservation on your website.
Receptionist	Under what name is your reservation, sir?[3]
Guest	It's under my name, Eric Pitt.
Receptionist	Let me check your reservation… Ah, here it is. You booked a deluxe room for two nights, so you are checking out on Saturday, right?
Guest	That's correct.
Receptionist	Did you request a nonsmoking room facing the ocean?
Guest	Yes, I did. Do you have one of those rooms on a high floor?
Receptionist	Let me see… Yes, we have a room available on the 10th floor. It is a nonsmoking room with an ocean view.
Guest	That sounds perfect.

Key & Alternative Expressions

1 I would like to check in, please.
= Can I check in?
= I have a reservation.

2 Do you have a reservation?
= Did you make a reservation?
= Have you made a reservation?
= Did you reserve a hotel room?

3 Under what name is your reservation, sir?
= May I have the name the reservation is under?
= What is the name?

B Check-in process II

04-02 

Receptionist	May I have your business card for registration, Mr. Pitt?
Guest	Oh, I don't have one with me now.
Receptionist	Then could you fill out this registration form?
Guest	Sure.
Receptionist	While you are filling out the registration form, may I have your credit card to make an imprint?
Guest	Here you go.
Receptionist	Thank you, Mr. Pitt. You're all set. Here is your room key. You can take the elevator on your right.
Guest	Thank you very much.
Receptionist	The bellman will take you up to your room. He will take care of your baggage as well. Checkout time is at noon. If you have any questions, press 0 on the room phone.
Guest	Wonderful!
Receptionist	Thank you, and enjoy your stay with us, sir.

Say the following sentences in English.

1 등록을 위해 명함을 받을 수 있을까요?

2 이 등록카드를 작성해주시겠습니까?

3 각인을 위해 신용카드를 받을 수 있을까요?

4 벨맨이 객실까지 모셔다드릴 것입니다.

5 문의 사항이 있으시면, 객실 전화로 0번을 눌러주십시오.

C Checking in walk-in guests

04-03 

Receptionist	Good evening, ma'am. Can I help you with anything?
Guest	Yes. I don't have a reservation. But do you have a room available for tonight?
Receptionist	I will check for you… We only have a deluxe room available for tonight. We can offer you that room at a rate of $280 a night plus tax and service charge.
Guest	Is that the best rate you can offer?
Receptionist	Yes, that's the best I can do for you, ma'am.
Guest	It looks like I have no choice. I guess I'll take it.
Receptionist	All right. May I have your picture ID and a credit card to secure the reservation, please?

Say the following sentences in English.

1 오늘밤 숙박 가능한 방 있습니까?

2 그 객실을 세금 및 봉사료 별도로 1박당 280달러에 제공해드릴 수 있습니다.

(Guest walks into the lobby late at night...)

Guest Hello. Can I check in? My name is David Ridgeway, and I made a reservation through an online travel agency.

Receptionist Just one moment, please. Let me check your reservation. How do you spell your last name?

Guest R-I-D-G-E-W-A-Y.

Receptionist Hmm… I'm very sorry, but we don't have a reservation under that name. Do you have a confirmation number?

Guest I'm afraid not.

Receptionist When did you make a reservation?

Guest About 2 hours ago.

Receptionist I see. Your reservation probably hasn't gotten through to our system yet. I will check you in now, and I will confirm your reservation as soon as the Reservation Department opens tomorrow. How long will you be staying?

Guest Three nights.

Receptionist Can I have your credit card to make an imprint, please?

Guest Sure, here it is.

Say the following sentences in English.

1 정말 죄송하지만, 고객님 성함으로 예약된 내역이 없습니다.

2 예약번호를 가지고 계십니까?

3 지금 체크인해드리고, 내일 예약부가 문을 여는 대로 고객님의 예약을 확정해드리겠습니다.

Essential Expressions   Check-In Service

1 Telling a guest a room rate

We can offer you a room at a rate of $200 a night plus [excluding] tax and service charge.

The rate is $200 per night, including tax and service charge.

It is $200 a night, and a 10% tax and service charge will be added to the rate.

2 Asking for a credit card to make an imprint

May I have your credit card to make an imprint?

Can I have your credit card to make an imprint of it?

May I have your credit card to imprint it?

3 Asking about a preferred type of room

What kind [type] of room would you like?

Would you prefer a nonsmoking or smoking room?

Do you have any preference for the room?

A Changing rooms

🎧 04-05

Agent: Front Desk Agent

Agent Front Desk. Ethan speaking. How may I help you, Ms. Gilmore?

Guest Hi. Is it possible to change my room?[1] I want to move closer to my friend's room. She is staying in room 605, and her name is Ashley Anderson. Do you have something like an adjoining room next to hers?[2]

Agent Let me check…. We have a room on the 6th floor, but it is not right next to her room. It is on the opposite side of the hall. Is that okay with you, Ms. Gilmore?

Guest That's fine. I will take it.

Agent All right, ma'am. When would you like to change rooms?

Guest Anytime is fine. I'm leaving in about half an hour and not coming back until late at night. I'd appreciate it if you would move my luggage while I'm out.[3]

Agent Certainly, ma'am. In that case, could you pack your belongings before you leave? I will send a bellman up to your room and have him move your stuff to the new room. But you don't need to pack the clothes hanging in the closet.

Guest Excellent! Thank you so much.

Agent Anytime, Ms. Gilmore.

Key & Alternative Expressions

1 **Is it possible to change my room?**

= Can I change my room?

= I'd like to change my room.

2 **Do you have something like an adjoining room next to hers?**

cf. Do you have two rooms close to each other?

Do you have connecting rooms?

Do you have a room on the same floor?

3 **I'd appreciate it if you would move my luggage while I'm out.**

= Will it be done until I'm back [till I return / till I come back]?

= Will it be done when [until / before / by the time] I get back?

Agent: Front Desk Agent

Agent   Front desk. Nicole speaking. Can I do anything for you, Mr. Simmons?

Guest   Hi. Do you provide a shuttle service for hotel guests to the downtown area?

Agent   Yes, we do, sir. We operate a courtesy shuttle bus between the hotel and downtown every hour. You can get detailed information at the concierge's desk.

Guest   That sounds good. What time is the last shuttle bus from here?

Agent   The last shuttle bus leaves the hotel at 9 P.M.

Guest   Oh, I see. Thank you for your assistance.

Agent   I'm happy to help, sir.

Say the following sentences in English.

1 호텔 투숙객에게 시내로 가는 셔틀 서비스를 제공합니까?

2 매시간 호텔과 시내를 오가는 무료 셔틀버스를 운행합니다.

3 마지막 셔틀버스는 오후 9시에 호텔에서 출발합니다.

Agent: Front Desk Agent

Agent   Good evening, sir. May I help you?

Guest   Good evening. I'm locked out of my room. I think I left the key in my room this morning.

Agent   May I have your name and room number?

Guest   My name is Henry Kwon. I'm in room 1030. Can you just make another key, please? I need one more for my wife as well.

Agent   Certainly, Mr. Kwon. Could I see some picture ID, please?

Guest   Here you go.

Agent   Thank you, sir. Here are your room keys.

Say the following sentences in English.

1 문이 잠겨서 방에 못 들어가고 있습니다.

2 사진이 나온 신분증을 보여주시겠습니까?

D Guest inquiries about hotel facilities

04-08

Agent: Front Desk Agent

Agent	Good morning, Ms. Wilson. How can I help you?
Guest	Hello. Is there a swimming pool in this hotel?
Agent	Yes, it is. It is in the fitness club on the 3rd floor. You can also find a gym, a sauna, a barbershop, and a beauty salon in it.
Guest	Can I use the pool for free?
Agent	Yes, Ms. Wilson. The pool and the gym are complimentary for all of our hotel guests.
Guest	Great. I'll definitely stop by to work out after breakfast. Where can I have breakfast?
Agent	You can have it at the cafe on the 1st floor. It serves breakfast from 5:30 A.M. to 10:00 A.M.
Guest	I'm in room 1212. Is breakfast included in the price?
Agent	Let me check on that, ma'am… Yes, your package includes a daily breakfast for two.

Say the following sentences in English.

1 수영장과 체육관은 모든 호텔 투숙객에게 무료입니다.

2 조식은 어디에서 먹을 수 있습니까?

3 카페는 오전 5시 30분부터 오전 10시까지 조식을 제공합니다.

4 조식이 가격에 포함되어 있습니까?

5 고객님이 패키지에는 일일 조식 2인분이 포함되어 있습니다.

E Extending a stay & providing an extra bed

04-09 

Agent: Front Desk Agent

Agent Good afternoon, sir. How may I help you?

Guest Hi. Can I extend my stay for another night?

Agent Absolutely. Let me check if the room is available. May I have your room number?

Guest Yes, I'm in room 804.

Agent Mr. Stewart, I extended your stay one more night.

Guest Great. By the way, can I request an extra bed in my room?

Agent Let me check the inventory… Yes, we have extra rollaway beds available now, sir. We can set one up for the additional charge of $20 per night. Would you like to use it?

Guest Yes, please. Thank you for your help.

Agent You're welcome, Mr. Stewart. Have a great day.

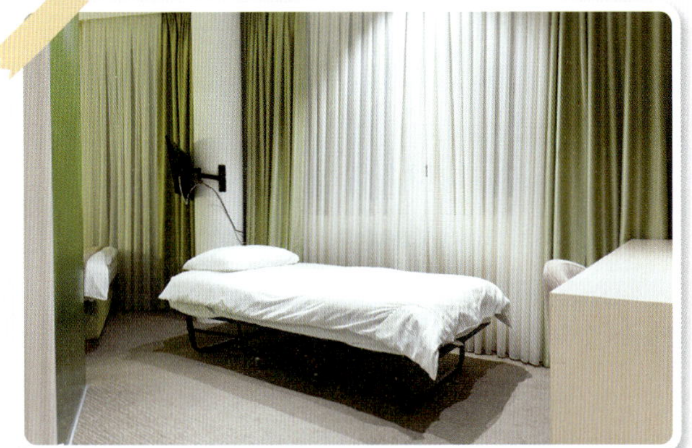

Say the following sentences in English.

1 투숙 기간을 하룻밤 더 연장할 수 있나요?

2 객실이 비는지 확인해보겠습니다.

3 투숙 기간을 1박 더 연장해드렸습니다.

4 제 방에 보조 침대를 요청할 수 있나요?

5 1박당 추가 요금 20달러에 보조 침대를 설치해드릴 수 있습니다

Essential Expressions   In-House Guest Service

1 Telling a guest the opening hours of a hotel's facilities

The café serves breakfast from 5:30 A.M. to 10:00 A.M.

Breakfast will be served from 5:30 A.M. to 10:00 A.M.

The restaurants stay open until 10:30 P.M.

The hours of operation are from 7:00 A.M. to 10:00 A.M.

2 Explaining about additional charges

We can set up an extra bed for the additional charge of $20 per night.

An additional charge will be added to your final bill.

You'll be charged for late checkout.

Exercises

A Choose the best response to each question.

1 Which of the following does NOT indicate the same thing as the others?

  ⓐ reservation

  ⓑ registration

  ⓒ check-in

2 Which is the main responsibility of a front desk agent?

  ⓐ checking in guests

  ⓑ picking up guests

  ⓒ escorting guests to their rooms

3 Where most likely does a walk-in guest check in to a hotel?

  ⓐ at a hotel front desk

  ⓑ on a hotel's website

  ⓒ at a travel agency

4 Which is NOT necessary to find a guest's reservation?

  ⓐ a confirmation number

  ⓑ the guest's last name

  ⓒ a credit card number

B Match each sentence with the best reply.

1 Under what name is the reservation?

2 Can I extend my stay for another night?

3 Can I check in, please?

4 You reserved a single room for five nights, right?

5 What time is breakfast served?

  ⓐ Do you have a reservation with us?

  ⓑ Let me check if the room is available.

  ⓒ That's correct.

  ⓓ You can have breakfast from 6 A.M. to 10 A.M.

  ⓔ It's under my name, Larry Wood.

C Complete the following conversation with the words in the box.

overlooking	imprint	choice	booked	confirmation

Guest Hello. I would like to check in, please. Here is my [1]____________ number.

Receptionist Thank you. Mr. Miller, you [2]____________ a deluxe room for 2 nights and requested a nonsmoking room with an ocean view, but I'm afraid that we don't have any available rooms [3]____________ the ocean now. How about a room with the pool view on a high floor instead?

Guest You leave me no [4]____________. I'll take it.

Receptionist Thank you, Mr. Miller. May I have your credit card to make a(n) [5]____________, please?

Guest Of course. Here you are.

Receptionist Okay, you are all set.

A Use the room tariffs below to practice checking in a walk-in guest. Take turns being a receptionist and a guest with your partner.

Room Tariffs

• Standard Rooms
Deluxe $200
Grand Deluxe $250

• Executive Rooms
Deluxe $300
Grand Deluxe $350

• Suites
Superior $500
Royal $800
Presidential $1,000

The above rates are subject to a 10% service charge and a 10% government tax.

Example

Receptionist   Good evening, sir. How may I assist you?

Guest   Do you have any rooms available for tonight?

Receptionist   ________________________

B Use the operation hours below to practice telling a guest the hours of operation of the hotel facilities. Take turns being a front desk agent and a guest with your partner.

Operation Hours

• Basement Floor
Flower Shop   09:00 A.M. - 08:00 P.M.
Drugstore   07:00 A.M. - 07:00 P.M.

• Lobby Floor
Coffee Shop   05:30 A.M. - 11:00 P.M.
Lobby Lounge   06:00 A.M. - 02:00 A.M.
Lobby Bar   06:00 P.M. - 02:00 A.M.

• 2nd Floor
Japanese Restaurant   12:00 P.M. - 02:30 P.M. / 06:00 P.M. - 10:00 P.M.
Chinese Restaurant   12:00 P.M. - 02:30 P.M. / 06:00 P.M. - 10:00 P.M.
Korean Restaurant   12:00 P.M. - 02:30 P.M. / 06:00 P.M. - 10:00 P.M.

• 3rd Floor
Fitness Club   05:30 A.M. - 09:30 P.M.

• 5th Floor
Business Center   07:00 A.M. - 10:00 P.M.

Example

Agent   Good afternoon, sir. May I help you?

Guest   When are the restaurants open?

Agent   ________________________

Front Desk

Located in the hotel lobby, the front desk is often considered the most important department in the hotel since it's the place where guests frequently  04-10 go. Guests approach the front desk in order to check in to and out of a hotel as well as to request information and assistance throughout their stay.

A warm welcome followed by quick and friendly service by the front desk agents can easily make the guests happy. That is why many guests consider them representatives of the hotel. The duties of front desk agents include registering guests, assigning rooms, issuing room keys, exchanging money, providing services for in-house guests, giving information, handling guest complaints, and checking guests out.

The requirements for the front desk agents are the following. First, they must have a positive and cheerful attitude with a smiley face to make any guests feel at ease. Second, they need to be physically healthy and energetic since they stand up during their entire shift. Third, they should be able to communicate well in as many foreign languages as possible, including English. Fourth, some computer skills, such as handling PMS (Property Management System), are required for this job. Lastly, they must be neat and well-groomed as they contact with guests in person.

📝 Words & Phrases

at ease relaxed

attitude the way you think and feel about something

complaint a statement in which you express your dissatisfaction

in-house guest a guest who is staying at a hotel

issue to publish, release, bring out, or print

lobby a hall near the entrance to a hotel

physically in a way that is related to a person's body

positive hopeful and confident; thinking of the good aspects of a situation rather than the bad ones

representative someone who represents a particular group

request to ask for something politely or formally

well-groomed clean and tidy; well cared for

05 Front Desk II (Cashier)

Warming Up

A Look at the picture below. What is happening? Share your thoughts with your partner.

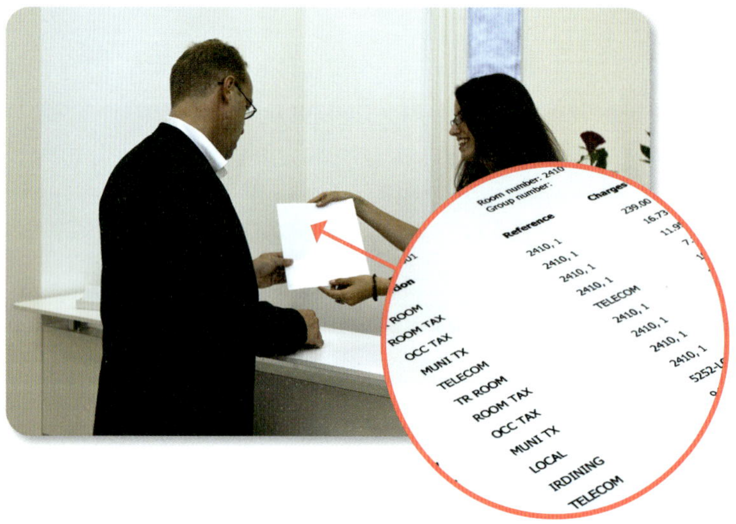

B Write the correct name of the payment method for each picture.

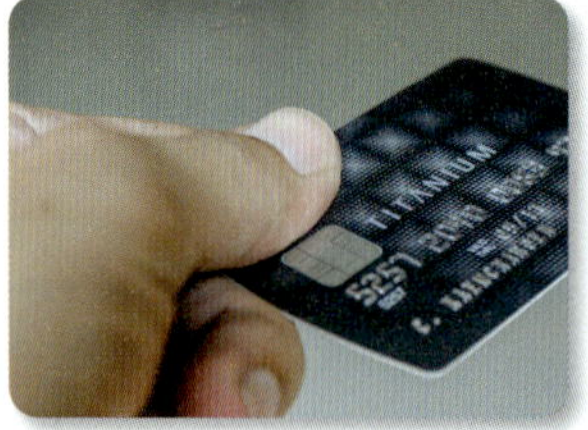   

1 _______________ 2 _______________ 3 _______________ 4 _______________

  Complete each sentence with the correct word or phrase from the box.

mistake	remove	look it over	settle	exchange	bill

1 Can you get my _____________ ready?

2 Please _____________ to see if everything is accurate.

3 I'll _____________ that charge from your bill immediately.

4 I'd like to _____________ U.S. dollars for Korean currency, please.

5 I apologize for the _____________. We will have this resolved as soon as possible.

6 I'm checking out now. I'd like to _____________ my bill, please.

Hotel Terminology Learn the following words and phrases used in the hotel industry.

account an arrangement with a hotel that allows a guest to buy goods now and to pay for them later

audit an examination of the financial records of a hotel to make sure that they are correct

exchange rate the rate at which one currency will be exchanged for another

incidental charge additional charges other than room charges; personal expenses

late checkout an arrangement that allows guests to check out later than they are supposed to leave

night auditor an employee in charge of the night audit

Tips to Know

Different Names of Front Desk Agents

Receptionist a front desk agent who registers guests, assigns rooms, issues keys, and gives guests information during their stays

Cashier a front desk agent who settles guests' accounts, breaks bills, and changes money for guests 

Night Clerk a front desk agent who handles the work of a receptionist, cashier, and night auditor while working the night [graveyard] shift

Night Auditor a front desk agent who conducts the night audit while working the night [graveyard] shift

A Preparing a checkout

🎧 05-01

Cashier: Front Desk Cashier

Cashier	Good morning. Front Desk. Carol speaking. How may I assist you?
Guest	Hello. I'm checking out in 10 minutes. Could you send someone up to my room to bring my baggage down to the lobby?[1]
Cashier	Certainly, Mr. Peterson. How many pieces of baggage do you have?
Guest	I have two suitcases, one box, and two bags.
Cashier	Our bellman will be there in a minute with a luggage cart. Is there anything else I can help you with?
Guest	Oh, yes. Could you call a cab to take me to the international airport? How much will the taxi fare be?
Cashier	There should be taxis waiting right outside the door at this time.[2] The fare will be about 80 dollars to the airport depending on traffic.[3]
Guest	Thank you for the information. Could you get my bill ready?[4]
Cashier	Sure, Mr. Peterson. Did you have anything from the minibar since last night?
Guest	Yes. I had one cola and two packages of chocolate chip cookies.
Cashie	Okay, I will add those to your bill. Did you have breakfast at the restaurant this morning?
Guest	No, I didn't. I ordered breakfast from room service.
Cashier	Okay. I will prepare your bill. Please come to the desk when you are ready.

Key & Alternative Expressions

1 **Could you send someone up to my room to bring my baggage down to the lobby?**
= Can you get someone to bring my baggage down to the lobby?
= Can you send someone to pick up my luggage?

2 **There should be taxis waiting right outside the door at this time.**
= There are always taxis outside at this time.

3 **The fare will be about 80 dollars to the airport depending on traffic.**
= It will cost around 80 dollars to the airport depending on traffic.

cf. The exact payment will depend on traffic.

4 **Could you get my bill ready?**
= Could I have my bill, please?
= Please prepare my bill.
= Will you make sure my bill is ready, please?

05-02

Cashier: Front Desk Cashier

Guest   Good morning. I'd like to check out, please.

Cashier   Okay. Let me help you with that, sir. What room were you in?

Guest   I was in room 1920. Here is my key.

Cashier   Thank you. Mr. Adams, how was your stay with us?

Guest   It was excellent as always.

Cashier   Did you use the minibar since last night?

Guest   No, I didn't use it at all.

Cashier   Let me print out your bill… It looks like you had breakfast at the cafe this morning, sir.

Guest   That's right.

Cashier   All right. Here is your bill. Your total is 350,000 won. Please look it over to see if everything is accurate.

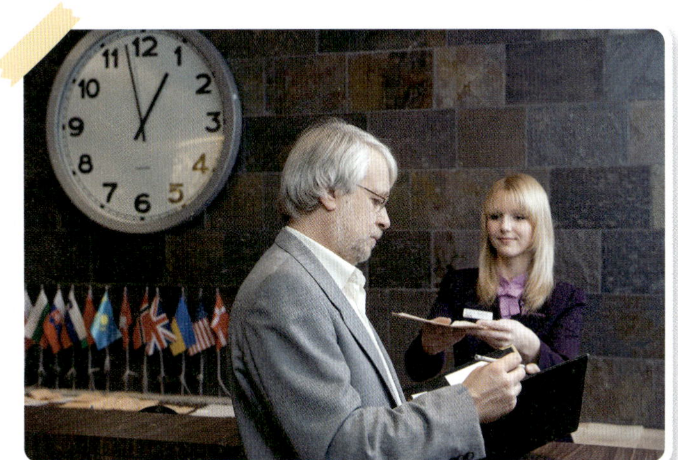

Say the following sentences in English.

1 제가 그것을 도와드리겠습니다.

2 몇 호실에 투숙하셨습니까?

3 투숙은 어떠셨습니까?

4 지난밤 이후로 미니바를 사용하셨습니까?

5 오늘 아침에 카페에서 조식을 드셨나 보네요.

6 총금액은 35만원입니다.

7 모두 정확한지 확인해주시기 바랍니다.

Cashier: Front Desk Cashier

Cashier	Would you like to pay now, Ms. Barnes?
Guest	Yes, please.
Cashier	Are you using the same credit card you gave me when you checked in?
Guest	Actually, can I pay with cash?
Cashier	Of course, ma'am.
Guest	How much do I owe?
Cashier	Your total comes to 220,000 won.
Guest	How much is that in U.S. dollars?
Cashier	It is 183 dollars and 30 cents.
Guest	Here is 200 dollars.
Cashier	Here is your change. It's 20,000 won. Thank you for staying with us, Ms. Barnes. I hope to see you again soon.

Say the following sentences in English.

1 체크인할 때 주신 신용카드를 사용하시겠습니까?

2 현금으로 결제해도 되나요?

3 다 해서 22만원 되겠습니다.

4 미국 달러로는 얼마인가요?

5 여기 거스름돈입니다. 2만원입니다.

Cashier: Front Desk Cashier

Cashier Good morning. How may I help you?

Guest Good morning. I'm supposed to leave today, but my flight doesn't depart until late evening. Can I stay in my room until this afternoon? I'm in room 1202.

Cashier Let me check if the room is available first… Yes, the room is available tonight, Mr. Hunt. You can stay in your room until 6 P.M., but will be charged 50% of the room rate.

Guest I see. If I check out before noon, can I leave my luggage somewhere in the hotel?

Cashier Certainly, sir. You can leave your luggage at the bell desk over there. The bellmen will be happy to take care of it for you, sir.

Guest That's good. I'll do that.

Cashier Oh, it's almost noon already. If you need some more time to pack your luggage, I can extend your checkout around 30 minutes at no extra charge.

Guest That sounds perfect! I appreciate it.

Cashier You're welcome, sir.

Say the following sentences in English.

1 먼저 객실이 비는지 확인해보겠습니다.

2 오후 6시까지 객실에 계실 수 있지만, 객실 요금의 50%가 청구됩니다.

3 정오 전에 체크아웃하면 호텔 어딘가에 짐을 맡길 수 있나요?

4 짐을 챙기는 데 시간이 좀 더 필요하시면, 체크아웃 시각을 30분 정도 무료로 연장해드릴 수 있습니다.

Essential Expressions Checkout Service

1 Asking about payment

Are you using the same credit card you gave me when you checked in?

Do you want to charge everything to your Visa card?

Are you paying by credit card?

How would you like to pay (your bill)?

2 Asking if guests enjoyed their stay

How was your stay (with us)?

How did you enjoy your stay (with us)?

Were there any inconveniences during your stay?

Did you enjoy your stay with us?

3 Saying farewell to guests

Thank you for staying with us.

I hope to see you again soon.

We hope you enjoyed your stay here and would be happy to welcome you back soon.

We hope you'll come and stay with us again. Have a safe trip back home.

It was a pleasure having you with us. We look forward to welcoming you again soon.

A Handling disputed charges

05-05

Cashier: Front Desk Cashier

Cashier Here is your bill. Please look it over to see if everything is correct.[1]

Guest Oh, thank you. Let me see… I think there are some mistakes on my bill.[2] I seem to have been charged for using the minibar, but I didn't take anything from it.

Cashier Let me check the details… They were a toothbrush, toothpaste, and a razor.

Guest Weren't they complimentary?

Cashier I'm sorry, but we charge for everything inside the minibar. Free toiletries are no longer provided to reduce the use of disposable products. They are included on the price list of the minibar as well.

Guest I see… There is another problem here. This charge from the bar must be wrong. I didn't stop by the bar at all during my stay.

Cashier I'll check the receipt. Please wait a moment… Here it is. Mr. Hill, room 620…

Guest That's neither my name nor my room number. I was in room 1620.

Cashier Yes, you're right. I'm very sorry for the mistake, Mr. Hall. I'll remove that charge from your bill immediately.[3]

Guest Okay.

Cashier Here is your new bill. Once again, I apologize for the error.

Key & Alternative Expressions

1 Please look it over to see if everything is correct.
= Please have a look at this printout.
= Please check it over to make sure that everything is accurate.

2 I think there are some mistakes on my bill.
= There is something wrong with my bill.
= My bill is incorrect.
= My bill isn't right.

3 I'll remove that charge from your bill immediately.
= I will deduct that charge from your bill immediately.
= I will adjust your bill immediately.
= I will take that [those] off and make a new bill for you.

cf. I will add that [those] to your bill.

Cashier: Front Desk Cashier

Guest	Can I settle my bill now? I'm checking out early tomorrow morning.
Cashier	Certainly. May I have your name and room number, please?
Guest	I'm Tanya Ross in room 1520, and I didn't use the minibar.
Cashier	All right, Ms. Ross. Let me print out your bill… Here you go. Please check it over to make sure everything is correct.
Guest	Okay… It looks right to me.
Cashier	Great. How would you like to pay, ma'am?
Guest	By credit card, please. Here it is.
Cashier	I'm sorry, but your card was declined. Do you have another one?
Guest	Oh, really? Do you take American Express?
Cashier	Yes, we do. We accept all major credit cards.

Say the following sentences in English.

1 모두 맞는지 확인해주시기 바랍니다.

2 결제는 어떻게 하시겠습니까?

3 죄송하지만, 카드 승인이 거절되었습니다. 다른 카드 있으십니까?

C **Exchanging money**   ⌒ 05-07

Cashier: Front Desk Cashier

Guest	I'd like to exchange U.S. dollars for Korean currency, please. What's the rate today?
Cashier	Today's exchange rate is 1,100 won to the dollar. How much would you like to change?
Guest	300 dollars, please.
Cashier	How would you like your bills, sir?
Guest	I want some 50,000 won bills and some 10,000 won bills.
Cashier	Very good, sir. May I have your passport and room number, please?

Say the following sentences in English.

1 오늘 환율은 1달러에 1,100원입니다.

2 얼마 환전하시겠습니까?

3 지폐는 어떻게 드릴까요?

Cashier: Front Desk Cashier

Cashier	Are you leaving one day earlier than expected?
Guest	That's right. My schedule has changed.
Cashier	Your room charge will be put on your company account, Mr. Logan. Here is your itemized bill for the incidental charges.
Guest	Everything looks fine. Here's my credit card.
Cashier	Thank you. How did you enjoy your stay, sir?
Guest	Actually, I was not very satisfied with your hotel this time.
Cashier	I'm sorry to hear that, sir. Were there any problems with your room?
Guest	Because of the noise from the next door, I woke up several times in the middle of the night.
Cashier	Oh, please accept my apologies, Mr. Logan. The guests next door to you were having a bridal shower. I'll put a note in your profile and make sure you get a quieter room the next time you're here.
Guest	Okay, thank you.
Cashier	I assure you it won't happen again on your next visit. If you feel any discomfort during your stay, please let us know at any time. We will take care of it immediately.
Guest	I'll do that. Thank you.

> **Say the following sentences in English.**

1 예정보다 하루 일찍 떠나십니까?

2 객실 요금은 고객님의 회사 계좌로 청구될 예정입니다.

3 여기 부대 비용에 대한 항목별 계산서입니다.

4 고객 프로파일에 메모를 달아두겠습니다.

5 다음에 방문하시면 이런 일 없을 겁니다.

Essential Expressions   **Handling Disputed Charges & Other Cashiering Services**

1 Telling a guest that a payment failed

I'm sorry, but your card was declined. / This card is not going through.

I'm afraid this card has expired. / I'm afraid this card is no longer valid.

I'm sorry, but this card is over the credit limit. / Your card was declined because you have exceeded your credit limit.

2 Explaining about incidental charges

They were a toothbrush, toothpaste, and a razor.

That's for the room service you ordered for lunch yesterday.

There is an international phone call charge on your bill.

You were charged for two cans of beer.

3 Apologizing politely

I apologize for the error [inconvenience]. / Please accept my apology.

A Choose the best response to each question.

1 Which is NOT the main responsibility of a front desk agent?

   (a) checking out guests

   (b) exchanging money

   (c) taking breakfast orders

2 Which is NOT necessary to exchange money?

   (a) a checkout date

   (b) a passport

   (c) a room number

3 What does a front desk agent need to check when settling a guest's bill?

   (a) the minibar usage of a guest since last night

   (b) the plate number of a guest's car

   (c) the baggage tag number of a guest

4 What would a front desk agent FIRST say to a guest when he or she complains of a problem with the bill?

   (a) We do apologize for our mistakes.

   (b) Please have a look at this printout.

   (c) Let me check the details.

B Match each sentence with the best reply.

1 How was your stay with us?

2 How much do I owe?

3 Can I leave my luggage somewhere?

4 I think my bill is incorrect.

5 Do you take MasterCard?

   (a) Your total comes to 200,000 won.

   (b) Let me check the detailed bill.

   (c) It was excellent!

   (d) You may leave it at the bell desk.

   (e) Yes, we do. We take all major credit cards.

C Complete the following conversation with the words in the box.

paying	staying	number	check	prepare

Guest   I'm checking out now. Could you [1] __________ my bill, please?

Cashier   Absolutely, ma'am. May I have your room [2] __________ please?

Guest   I was in room 1030. Here is my key. I didn't use the minibar.

Cashier   Here is your bill. Please look it over to [3] __________ that everything is correct.

Guest   Everything looks good.

Cashier   How will you be [4] __________ ?

Guest   Here is my credit card.

Cashier   Thank you. Please sign here... Here is your receipt. Thank you for [5] __________ with us.

Use the guest folio below to practice checking out a guest and handling disputed charges. Take turns being a front desk cashier and a guest with your partner.

Guest Folio

Date	Description	Amount
6/20/19	Room charge	200,000
6/20/19	Room service charge	20,000
6/20/19	Government tax	22,000
6/20/19	Airport pickup service	110,000
6/20/19	Lobby bar	56,000
6/20/19	Korean restaurant	109,000
6/20/19	Pay TV	11,000
6/21/19	Room charge	200,000
6/21/19	Room service charge	20,000
6/21/19	Government tax	22,000
6/21/19	Café	76,000
6/21/19	Chinese restaurant	98,000
6/21/19	Business center	55,000
6/22/19	Airport drop-off service	100,000

Total Due KW 1,099,000
Total Paid KW 0

Example

Cashier	Good morning, sir. Are you checking out now?
Guest	Yes, I am. Can I see my bill, please?
Cashier	....

Read the following passage that describes what the front desk cashier does.

Front Desk Cashier

The two major jobs of front desk agents are checking guests out (cashiering) and checking guests in (reception). However, no front desk agent is specifically assigned to do either job. Each of the agents at the front desk can be a receptionist or cashier depending on guests' requests. Normally, the checkout time is at noon, and the check-in time is at 3 P.M. Therefore, the morning shift agents usually do cashiering while the afternoon shift agents usually do registration.

If a guest leaves after the checkout time, the hotel usually charges the guest an additional charge for late checkout. The late checkout fee varies from a certain percentage of a room rate to a full charge for a day, depending on the time of the requested late checkout.

Express checkout is a way to check out without stopping by the front desk. Guests can either check their itemized bill by using an on-screen display on an in-room TV, or they can have the bill placed under their door the night before they check out. Guests only have to have left their credit card to make an imprint of it at the front desk when they checked in.

📝 Words & Phrases

assign to give a job

cashier an employee who guests pay money to

charge to ask someone to pay money

display a screen; an arrangement of things that have been put in a particular place

itemized bill a list of charges

job work

major more important, serious, or significant than other things

place to put

shift a particular period of work time during the day or night

stop by to visit a place for a short amount of time

vary to be different

UNIT

06 Concierge & GRO Desk

Warming Up

A Look at the picture below. Who is she? What does she do? Share your thoughts with your partner.

B Choose the picture that is NOT related to a concierge's duties.

try	interested in	describe	recommend	operate	on foot	attending	admission fee

1 Could you _______________ some nice places for shopping?

2 Why don't you _______________ our hotel restaurant?

3 It will take about 10 minutes _______________.

4 Which conference are you _______________?

5 I am _______________ Korean history and culture.

6 They _______________ from 9 A.M. to 6 P.M.

7 The _______________ is included in the ticket price.

8 Can you _______________ your lost mobile phone?

Hotel Terminology Learn the following words and phrases used in the hotel industry.

ballroom a large banquet room used for conferences, wedding ceremonies, and social meetings in a hotel

continental breakfast a simple breakfast that consists of bread and coffee or tea

corridor a long passage in a building, especially with rooms on each side

express check-in/checkout special check-in or checkout service designed for VIP or special request guest

GRO guest relations officer, usually responsible for VIP guest treatment

Lost & Found a place where lost property is kept, or the relevant service

video conferencing system a type of technology that enables people from multiple locations to have a conference without actually meeting in person

Tips to Know

Lost and Found

The lost and found service can be handled by two departments according to the place the lost items were found.

Place Items Were Found	Department in Charge
In a hotel's public areas, such as the lobby, restaurants, or banquet rooms	Concierge
In guest rooms	Housekeeping

A Recommending tourist attractions

⌒ 06-01

Concierge Good morning, sir. How may I help you?

Guest Hi. This is my first visit to Korea. Could you recommend some famous places to visit in Seoul?[1]

Concierge Well. There are so many popular tourist sites in Seoul. What kind of place would you like to visit?

Guest I'm very interested in Korean history and culture.[2]

Concierge Well… Then you should definitely visit Gyeongbokgung, the main royal palace during the Joseon Dynasty.

Guest Oh, I think I've heard about it before.

Concierge If you want to get a glimpse of Korean traditional life and culture, I would recommend visiting Namsangol Hanok Village.[3] You can actually learn all about Korean culture there. For instance, you can try *hanbok*, Korean traditional clothes, learn Hangeul calligraphy, the Korean alphabet, and take Korean traditional etiquette classes such as the tea ceremony. You can also try traditional games and take a guided tour of the hanok village area.

Guest Both places sound like a lot of fun! I'm really looking forward to visiting them.

Concierge For your information, those two places are close to each other. It only takes about 10 minutes by taxi from the palace to the hanok village.

Guest Excellent! How much is the admission fee at each place?

Concierge The entrance fee for Gyeongbokgung is 3,000 won, and the hanok village has no entrance fee.

Key & Alternative Expressions

1 Could you recommend some famous places to visit in Seoul?
= Can you suggest some nice places in Seoul?
= Can you give me some advice for traveling Seoul?

2 I'm very interested in Korean history and culture.
= I have interest in your history and culture.
= I'm curious to know about Korean history and culture.

3 I would recommend visiting Namsangol Hanok Village.
= Why don't you visiting Namsangol Hanok Village?
= How about visiting Namsangol Hanok Village?
= You should definitely visit Namsangol Hanok Village.
= I suggest visiting Namsangol Hanok Village.
= I suggest you visit Namsangol Hanok Village.
= You can't miss Namsangol Hanok Village.

Guest	I'd like to have some Korean food. Can you recommend a good restaurant?
Concierge	We have a Korean restaurant on the 2nd floor. It has some good authentic Korean food.
Guest	I've already been there. I want to try another place this time.
Concierge	In that case, there is a place called Hansarang near the hotel. It's only a 10-minute walk from here. And there is another restaurant called K-Garden. It'll take about 20 minutes by taxi to get there. They both operate from 11 A.M. to 11 P.M.
Guest	How is the food at each place?
Concierge	The food at both places is great. But the menus are a little different. Hansarang is an authentic Korean food restaurant while K-Garden is famous for its meat dishes such as *bulgogi* and *galbi*. If you love meat, I would recommend K-Garden. You can also enjoy shopping after lunch. The restaurant is located on Garosu-gil, and the area has many trendy stores and open-air cafes.
Guest	Oh, that's nice. Then I will choose K-Garden.
Concierge	Would you like me to make a reservation for you?
Guest	That would be wonderful

Say the following sentences in English.

1 여기서 걸어서 10분 거리밖에 안 됩니다.

2 제가 예약을 해드릴까요?

Guest	Excuse me, but I lost my wallet somewhere in the lobby. Who should I talk to?
Concierge	I can help you with that, sir. When did you lose it?
Guest	Just now, I guess. I was in the lobby about an hour ago, and then I went to the coffee shop to meet my friend. When I met him, I realized I didn't have my wallet in my pocket.
Concierge	I'm sorry to hear that, sir. Can you describe what it looks like?
Guest	It is a brown leather wallet. It has a big letter B on the front.
Concierge	All right. Let me check the list of lost items, sir… Oh, here it is. Let me get it from the back.
Guest	Oh, thank you very much.
Concierge	My pleasure.

Say the following sentences in English.

1 어떻게 생겼는지 설명해주시겠습니까?

2 뒤에서 그것을 가져오겠습니다.

Guest	I need to buy some souvenirs for my family. I also want to visit a Korean traditional market. Is there any place I can do both?
Concierge	Of course, ma'am. There are Namdaemun Market and Dongdaemun Market. They are two of the biggest traditional markets in Seoul.
Guest	So… Are they pretty much the same?
Concierge	Not really, ma'am. Namdaemun Market is more traditional than Dongdaemun Market. There are many street vendors at Namdaemun Market while there are many modern shopping malls at Dongdaemun Market.
Guest	I want to visit both of them. Can I visit them by subway? I really want to take the subway in Seoul.
Concierge	Certainly. Here is a map of Seoul. A subway map is on the back. You are here, and Dongdaemun Market is right here at Dongdaemun History & Culture Park Station. Turn left as soon as you go through the hotel's revolving door, and walk straight for about 5 minutes. You'll see the subway station right in front of you.

> **Say the following sentences in English.**

1 가족에게 줄 기념품을 좀 사야 합니다.

2 남대문시장에는 노점상이 많은 반면, 동대문시장에는 현대적인 쇼핑몰이 많습니다.

3 호텔 회전문을 통과하시자마자 좌회전하셔서 5분 정도 직진하십시오.

4 바로 앞에 지하철역이 보이실 겁니다.

Essential Expressions 　Concierge Service

1 Asking a guest's interests

What kind of place would you like to visit?

What are you interested in?

Do you have any particular place in mind?

2 Telling the distance and time required to get to a destination

It's (only) a 10-minute walk from here.

It takes about 15 minutes on foot.

It takes about 20 minutes by walking.

It'll take about 5 minutes by car.

It is within walking distance.

It's a bit far.

A Checking in VIP guests

🎧 06-05 

(A VIP guest's car arrives at the hotel.)

GRO Welcome back, Ms. Lane. I'm Gary, a GRO. Let me escort you to your room.[1]
Your luggage will be delivered to your room shortly.

Guest Thank you. Your service is excellent as always.[2]

GRO My pleasure, Ms. Lane. This way, please…

(In the elevator…)

GRO We've given you a room on the 15th floor as usual.

Guest Oh, you remembered that is my favorite floor. Did you set up a laptop in my room?

GRO Absolutely, Ms. Lane. We also set up a printer according to your request.

Guest Thank you.

(Both get off the elevator.)

GRO Here we are. After you, Ms. Lane. Your room is on the right. This is your room.

(They open the door and go in.)

GRO (After showing the room to the guest) Here is your room key.
Do you need anything else?

Guest Not right now. Thank you.

GRO Very good, Ms. Lane. Please dial 101 on your room
phone if you need anything.[3] You'll be able to reach
the guest relations officer desk any time from 7 A.M.
to 10 P.M.

Key & Alternative Expressions

1 Let me escort you to your room.
= I'll take you to your room.
= Let me walk you to your room.
= I'll show you to your room.

2 Your service is excellent as always.
= Your service is excellent as usual.
= I'm always pleased with your service.

3 Please dial 101 on your room phone if you need anything.
= Please call me if you need me.
= Please let us [me] know if you need anything.
= Please do not hesitate to contact us if you need any further assistance.
= Please feel free to contact me if you have any further questions.

GRO	Thank you for calling. This is GRO. Amanda speaking. How may I assist you?
Guest	Hi, Amanda. I'm Greg Simmons in room 1512. I'd like to book a conference room for tomorrow.
GRO	Okay… Could you give me some details, please?
Guest	I'll need a conference room equipped with a videoconferencing system at 7:00 tomorrow morning. Five people will attend the conference. If we could, we would like to have breakfast while we have the conference.
GRO	We can do that for you, Mr. Simmons. What would you like to order for breakfast?
Guest	A continental breakfast for five will do. Please make sure that there are toast, orange juice, and coffee.
GRO	I see. I'll arrange a video conference for 7 o'clock tomorrow morning with five continental breakfasts. Do you have anything else to request?
Guest	No, that's it for now.
GRO	All right, Mr. Simmons. Please let me know if you have any further requests.

Say the following sentences in English.

1 자세한 사항을 말씀해주시겠습니까?

2 내일 아침 7시에 화상 회의 설비를 갖춘 회의실이 필요합니다.

3 토스트, 오렌지 주스, 커피를 반드시 준비해주십시오.

4 내일 아침 7시 정각에 화상 회의와 유럽식 조식 5인분을 준비해놓겠습니다.

5 그 밖에 더 요청하실 것이 있으면 알려주십시오.

Teacher's note 빵의 종류

Wheat Bread (밀빵)

	• 밀가루로 만드는 가장 일반적인 빵 • 글루텐 함량이 높아 빵이 잘 부풀고 탄력이 좋음
White Bread (흰빵)	• 밀의 겉껍질(bran)와 배아(germ)를 제거한 정제된 밀가루(flour)로 만들어 부드럽고 폭신한 질감을 나타냄
Whole Wheat Bread (통밀빵)	• 밀의 겉껍질과 배아를 제거하지 않고 밀알 전체를 갈아 만든 통밀가루(whole wheat flour)로 만들어지며, 섬유질과 영양소가 보다 풍부함

Rye Bread (호밀빵)

• 호밀가루(rye flour)를 주로 사용해 만들며, 밀가루와 혼합하기도 함
   cf. 호밀은 보드카, 위스키, 맥주 제조 과정에서도 사용
• 글루텐 함량이 밀빵에 비해 낮아 상대적으로 빵이 더 조밀하고 촉촉하며 쫄깃한 질감을 가짐
• 특유의 진하고 구수한 맛과 약간의 신맛이 특징임

Guest	Pardon me. I'm here to attend a conference. Where is the conference room?
GRO	Which conference are you attending, ma'am? We have many different conferences taking place now.
Guest	Here is my invitation.
GRO	Let me see… Your conference will be held in the grand ballroom on the 2nd floor. It is scheduled to start at 2 P.M. You can take the escalator on your left. You may also take the stairs or elevator on your right.
Guest	Thank you. By the way, where is the restroom?
GRO	Go straight toward the coffee shop. Then, turn right and go to the end of the hall. The restroom will be on your left. You can't miss it.

> **Say the following sentences in English.**

1 고객님의 회의는 2층 그랜드볼룸에서 열립니다.

2 회의는 오후 2시에 시작할 예정입니다.

3 커피숍 쪽으로 직진하십시오.

4 우회전하셔서 복도 끝까지 가십시오.

5 찾기 쉬우실 겁니다.

Teacher's note	화장실을 뜻하는 영어 단어
Restroom	• 📜 주로 공공 장소(public place)나 식당, 쇼핑몰 등에서 많이 사용
Bathroom	• 집이나 호텔 등 개인 공간에서 주로 사용되며 미국에서 화장실을 뜻하는 가장 일반적인 표현
Toilet	• 🇬🇧 화장실, 변기 📜 변기 • 영국, 호주 등 국가에서 흔히 사용하며 공공 화장실을 지칭 (미국에서는 다소 직설적으로 들릴 수 있음)
Ladies' room/ Men's room	• 여성용/남성용 화장실을 구분할 때 사용
Washroom	• 캐나다와 미국 일부지역에서 주로 쓰이는 공공 화장실 표현
Powder room	• 주로 여성용 화장실을 정중하고 약간 우아하게 부를 때 사용
Lavatory	• 비행기, 기차 등에 있는 화장실을 뜻하는 격식 있는 표현
WC	• Water Closet의 약자 • 예전에 쓰이던 표현으로 표지판이나 도면 등에서 볼 수 있었던 유럽식 표현
the john	• 📜 속어로서 공식적인 자리에서는 사용하지 않음 (16세기 말 수세식 변기를 처음 고안한 영국의 존 해링턴(John Harington) 경의 이름에서 유래)
the loo	• 🇬🇧 속어로서 공식적인 자리나 미국에서는 사용하지 않음
Sample Expression	• Where is the restroom? = Where can I wash my hands? = Is there any place I can wash up?

(A GRO approaches a guest checking out with a friendly smile.)

GRO Good morning, sir. Are you leaving now?

Guest Yes, I am.

GRO You can check out over here. Come this way, please…

Guest Okay.

GRO How was your stay, sir?

Guest Well, everything was excellent, except for one thing.

GRO What was the problem, sir?

Guest My room was really cold. I tried to adjust the temperature and got an extra blanket, but the room was still freezing.

GRO I apologize for the inconvenience. The rooms located on both ends of the corridor tend to be colder than the others. I'll put a note on your profile so that you can get a room in the middle on your next visit.

Guest Thank you.

GRO Are you going to Incheon International Airport?

Guest Yes, I am.

GRO Do you have transportation to the airport?

Guest I'm going to take a taxi.

GRO Let me arrange a taxi and have a bellman put your baggage into the trunk while you settle the bill.

Guest That would be nice. Thank you very much.

GRO We hope you come and stay with us again. Have a safe trip back home, sir.

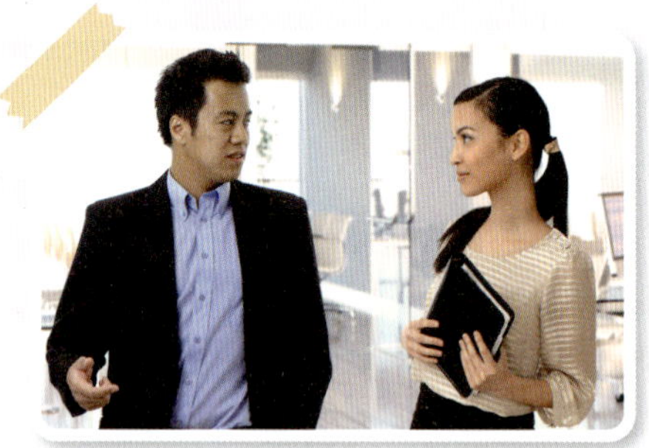

> **Say the following sentences in English.**

1 복도 양 끝에 위치한 객실이 다른 객실보다 추운 경향이 있습니다.

2 제가 고객 프로파일에 메모를 달아서 다음 번 방문하실 때는 중앙에 있는 객실을 배정받으실 수 있도록 하겠습니다.

3 고객님께서 정산하시는 동안, 택시를 준비하고 벨맨을 시켜 짐을 트렁크에 넣겠습니다.

Essential Expressions **GRO (Guest Relations Officer) Service**

1 Saying that a service will be ready

I'll arrange a video conference. / I'll prepare eight continental breakfasts.

I'll organize personal training sessions in the fitness club. / I'll book a dinner reservation for you.

2 Promising guests better services on their next visit

I'll put a note on your profile so that you can get a room in the middle on your next visit.

I'll leave a note in your profile for my colleagues to double-check the smell in your room on your next stay.

I'll make sure to put a note on your profile to avoid a squeaky bed in the future.

I'll make a note in your profile that you prefer a quieter room.

Exercises

A Choose the best response to each question.

1 Which department does a concierge belong to?
  ⓐ Food & Beverage
  ⓑ Rooms
  ⓒ Back Office

2 Who is in charge of taking care of VIP guests and handling their complaints?
  ⓐ a concierge
  ⓑ a cashier
  ⓒ a GRO

3 Who is in charge of express check-in service for VIP guests?
  ⓐ a front desk agent
  ⓑ a bellhop
  ⓒ a GRO

4 Which is NOT a duty of a concierge?
  ⓐ exchanging foreign currency
  ⓑ advising guests about tour programs
  ⓒ handling lost and found items

B Match each sentence with the best reply.

1 What are you interested in? •   • ⓐ I'm interested in art and music.

2 How much is the admission fee? •   • ⓑ It takes about 10 minutes by car.

3 How long does it take? •   • ⓒ That's it for now.

4 Do you have anything else to request? •   • ⓓ Everything was excellent!

5 How was your stay? •   • ⓔ It's free.

C Complete the following conversation with the words in the box.

floor	advice	admission	open	visit

Concierge	Good morning, ma'am. How may I assist you?
Guest	Hello. I'd like to do some sightseeing in Seoul. Could you give me some [1]__________?
Concierge	N Seoul Tower is a nice place to [2]__________. It is located at the top of Mt. Namsan. It has an observatory on the third [3]__________. You can enjoy great panoramic views of the city up there.
Guest	That sounds wonderful! When is the observatory [4]__________?
Concierge	The observatory deck is open from 10 A.M. to 11 P.M. The [5]__________ fee is 10,000 won.

Role-Playing

Use the floor plan of a hotel below to practice giving directions to a guest. Take turns being a GRO and a guest with your partner. Use the expressions in the box if needed.

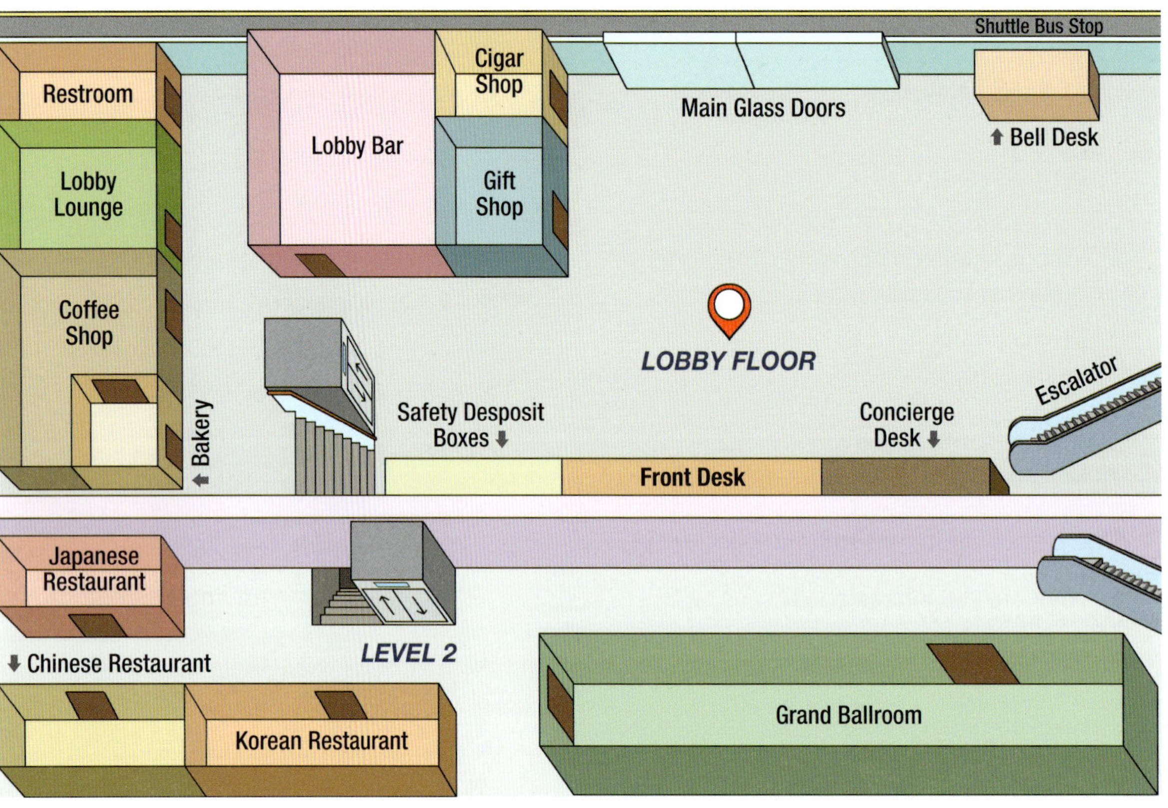

Example

GRO Good afternoon, ma'am. May I help you?

Guest Yes. Where is the Korean restaurant?

GRO Take the elevator over there to the 2nd floor. When you get out, you will see the Korean restaurant in front of you.

Giving Directions

______________ is **over there**.

Go straight toward ______________.

Go between ______________ and ______________.

Go down the hallway **until you see** ______________ on your left.

Walk straight down this corridor. It will be on your right.

Walk along this corridor and **take the first left**.

Walk down the hallway and turn right **after** ______________.

Keep walking to ______________, and then turn right.

When you come to ______________, turn left.

You'll find ______________ on the right, **just [past / before]** ______________.

______________ is **at the end of** the hallway on the left.

It's **on the** ______________ floor.

Go [upstairs / downstairs].

Take the [elevator / escalator] to the ______________ floor.

When you **go out of** the elevator, ______________.

When you **get out**, ______________.

From ______________, **walk across** the lobby.

Walk through the doors and then immediately turn left.

It is **straight ahead of** you.

It is **[in front of / opposite / next to / behind]** ______________.

Concierges and GROs

🎧 06-09

A concierge assists guests with almost everything throughout their stays. He recommends local attractions, shopping places, restaurants, and transportation. He makes booking arrangements as well. He not only makes reservations for restaurants, sightseeing tours, and transportation for guests, but he also books tickets for plays, sporting events, and any other activities they want to do. Since a concierge is frequently asked questions about the area's best spots, history, and culture, he has to be knowledgeable about the city where the hotel is located. A concierge also handles inquiries regarding lost and found items and lends guests wheelchairs and strollers.

While one of the main responsibilities of a concierge is to provide guests with information about the hotel's facilities and services as well as local travel for guests, the most important duty of a GRO is to serve VIP guests. A GRO performs express check-in and secretarial services for VIP guests during their stays. A GRO also handles all types of requests, questions, and complaints from guests as a one-stop service. In addition, a GRO stands by in the lobby to welcome arriving guests and says farewell to departing guests. When the hotel is very busy, a GRO even supports his colleagues from other departments such as the front desk, concierge desk, and the Executive Floor Department.

A hotel concierge and a GRO must be fit, stay cheerful and patient, have good manners, and be fluent in as many foreign languages as possible in order to act as a qualified personal assistant to the guests.

📝 **Words & Phrases**

arrangement plans or preparations to make something happen

assist to help someone by doing something for that person

cheerful friendly and pleasant in behavior

knowledgeable knowing a lot about something

lend to give something for a short time, expecting it to be given back

patient able to wait a long time

perform to do something

recommend to suggest that something is good or useful

regarding about; concerning

secretarial relating to the work of a secretary

sightseeing traveling to interesting places that tourists usually visit

stroller a small chair on wheels in which a baby or small child can sit and be wheeled around

UNIT 07 Executive Floor

Warming Up

A Look at the picture below. Have you ever heard about executive floors in a hotel? What do you know about them? Share your thoughts with your partner.

B What does the room rate for executive floors usually include? Check the correct boxes.

ⓐ breakfast	☐	ⓑ meeting room		☐
ⓒ dinner	☐	ⓓ happy hour		☐
ⓔ late checkout after 6 P.M.	☐	ⓕ fitness center		☐

  Complete each sentence with the correct word or phrase from the box.

all-day explain business card separate take a seat access billed along with

1 Why don't you ________________ while I check you in?

2 I'll need your ________________ to register your information.

3 Can you ________________ the benefits of staying on an executive club floor?

4 The executive lounge serves ________________ complimentary refreshments.

5 You can enjoy exclusive ________________ to the executive lounge.

6 Can you split the bill into two ________________ ones?

7 Complimentary breakfast is served in the executive lounge ________________ soft drinks and snacks.

8 I ordered room service and had it ________________ to my room.

Hotel Terminology Learn the following words and phrases used in the hotel industry.

executive floor a special floor at a hotel; club floor; club level; business floor

happy hour an EFL service; a period of the day when guests can have unlimited alcoholic beverages along with some finger foods and snacks (usually in the evening)

Tips to Know

The Key Services of Executive Floor Lounges

- Executive lounge express check-in and checkout service
- Free Internet access
- Complimentary breakfast
- All-day complimentary coffee and tea
- Complimentary alcoholic beverages, hors d'oeuvres, finger foods, and snacks during happy hour
- Free use of meeting rooms (Free hours may vary depends on hotels.)
- Complimentary ironing service (1-2 pieces)
- Shoeshine service
- Newspaper delivery service
- Complimentary access to the fitness center: gym, indoor swimming pool, and sauna

A EFL check-in service

Agent: Executive Floor Guest Service Agent

Agent	Good morning. Welcome to the Crimson Hotel. May I assist you?
Guest	Yes, I'm checking in.[1] My name is Luis Howard.
Agent	Sure, Mr. Howard. Would you please take a seat?[2] Okay… You have a reservation for three nights in an executive deluxe room with a double bed. Is that correct?
Guest	That's right. I'll be checking out on Saturday.
Agent	May I have your business card so that I can register your information?
Guest	No problem. Here you are.
Agent	How would you like to pay?
Guest	With my VISA card.
Agent	May I have your credit card to make an imprint?
Guest	Sure, here it is.
Agent	What time do you expect to check out on Saturday, sir?
Guest	Um… I'm thinking of checking out at around 2:30 P.M.
Agent	Let me extend your checkout time then. Will you need transportation to the airport?
Guest	Yes. Can you arrange it, please?
Agent	Sure. Could you tell me your departure time and the flight number, please?
Guest	It's at 5:30 P.M. I'll be on flight OZ123 departing from Incheon International Airport.
Agent	I see. I'll arrange a limousine to the airport. The fee will be billed to your room. You're all set, Mr. Howard. Here is your room key. Your room is on the 17th floor. Let me briefly explain about our EFL services. You can enjoy all-day refreshments in the lounge until 10 P.M. Happy hour runs from 5 P.M. to 8 P.M. Breakfast is served from 6:30 A.M. to 10:00 A.M. The meeting room is available for up to 2 hours a day. In addition, you have free access to our fitness center, which has a pool. May I have your luggage tag? I'll have your bags delivered to your room.
Guest	Here you go.
Agent	Enjoy your stay, Mr. Howard.

Key & Alternative Expressions

1 I am checking in.

= I am going to check in. = I will be checking in. = I would like to check in. = I'm ready to check in.

2 Would you please take a seat?

= Please have a seat so that I can register your information. = Would you please have a seat (while I check you in)?

⌒ 07-02

Agent: Executive Floor Guest Service Agent

Agent Good morning, Mr. Parker. Are you checking out?

Guest Yes. Can you prepare my bill while I am having breakfast? Here is my key. I took one beer from the minibar.

Agent Of course. Do you need assistance with your luggage?

Guest Yes, that would be great.

Agent Oh, you reserved a limousine to the airport for 10 A.M. I will get your limo ready and have a bellman bring your baggage down to the car. Enjoy your breakfast, Mr. Parker.

(15 minutes later…)

Guest Is my bill ready?

Agent Yes, Mr. Parker. Here is your bill. Please look it over to see if everything is correct.

Guest Everything looks fine. Can you make two separate bills for me? My company will only pay for the room, and I will take care of the rest.

Agent Certainly, Mr. Parker. Here they are.

Guest Perfect. I'll pay with my AMEX card.

Agent Okay, Mr. Parker. You are all set. Here are your separate bills and the receipts. Your luggage is already loaded in the limousine out front.

(The agent walks the guest to an elevator and presses the button to go down.)

Agent How was your stay, Mr. Parker?

Guest Oh, it was excellent as usual.

Agent I'm very pleased to hear that.

(The elevator doors finally open, and the guest gets in.)

Agent Have a nice trip back home, Mr. Parker. We're looking forward to seeing you again soon.

Say the following sentences in English.

1 제가 조식을 먹을 동안 계산서를 준비해주실 수 있습니까?

2 계산서를 두 개로 나누어주실 수 있습니까?

3 리무진을 대기시키고 벨맨을 시켜 짐을 차 있는 곳까지 내려드리겠습니다.

Essential Expressions   EFL Check-In & Checkout Service

1 Offering to help a checking-out guest
Do you need assistance with your luggage?
Would you like me to arrange transportation for you?

2 Helping a guest checking out with baggage and transportation
I will get your limo ready and have a bellman bring your baggage down to the car.
Let me have a cab waiting outside for you.

A EFL lounge service

🎧 07-03

Agent: Executive Floor Guest Service Agent

When a guest comes in after the breakfast hours

Guest	Can I have breakfast now?
Agent	I'm sorry, but the breakfast hours are over.[1]
Guest	What are the breakfast hours?[2]
Agent	Breakfast is from 6 A.M. to 10 A.M., ma'am.
Guest	Oh, I woke up late this morning. What can I do?
Agent	You can still order a continental breakfast by calling room service until 11 A.M. I can place an order for you if you want, ma'am.
Guest	That would be wonderful!

When a guest orders an alcoholic beverage after happy hour

Agent	Would you like to order something to drink, sir?
Guest	Yes. Can I have a glass of red wine, please? It's free, right?
Agent	I'm sorry, but alcoholic beverages are free of charge only during happy hour. If you would like to order one now, it will be charged to your room. Will that be all right, sir?
Guest	Oh, I didn't realize how late it was.[3] I'll just have a cola with ice.

Key & Alternative Expressions

1 I'm sorry, but the breakfast hours are over.

= I'm afraid that the breakfast hours are finished.

2 What are the breakfast hours?

= What time is breakfast served?

= What time does breakfast begin?

= What time does breakfast end?

3 I didn't realize how late it was.

= I totally lost of time.

= Oh, gosh, look at the time.

= My, how time files!

🎧 07-04

Agent: Executive Floor Guest Service Agent

Guest	I'd like to reserve a meeting room, please.
Agent	Sure. When would you like to use it?
Guest	I need it tomorrow from 1 P.M. to 4 P.M.
Agent	All right, ma'am. Please wait a moment while I check… Yes, it's available at that time. May I have your room number, please?
Guest	I'm staying in room 1816.
Agent	How many people will be using the meeting room?
Guest	There will be five people in total, including two from other hotels.
Agent	The meeting room is available free of charge for two hours per room. So you can use it for the entire 3 hours at no extra charge if you have another EFL guest in your group. Can you give me another person's name, Ms. Green?
Guest	Mr. Brandon Young is in our group, but I don't remember his room number.
Agent	No problem. Let me check for you… Okay, he is one of our executive guests. Is there anything else you need in the meeting room?
Guest	Yes, we would like to have the meeting over lunch. Can we order 5 club sandwiches and coffees, please? And charge everything to my room, please.
Agent	All right, ma'am. Will that be all?
Guest	Yes, that's it for now.
Agent	Thank you, Ms. Green. If you need anything else, please contact us on the executive floor.

Say the following sentences in English.

1 회의실을 예약하고 싶은데요.

2 언제 이용하려고 하십니까?

3 그때 이용하실 수 있습니다.

4 몇 분이 회의실을 이용하실 예정입니까?

5 회의실은 객실 하나당 2시간씩 무료로 이용하실 수 있습니다.

6 다른 분 성함을 말씀해주시겠습니까?

7 더 필요한 것이 있으시면 비지니스 전용층으로 연락 주십시오.

1   Asking the number of group members

How many people will be using the meeting room?

How many people will be coming?

How many people will be attending the meeting?

How many people are there in your group?

How large is your party?

How many are you?

May I have the number of guests?

2   Asking if there are any additional requests

Will that be all?

Is there anything else you need?

Is that everything?

3   Telling guests what to do if they need additional requests

If you need anything else, please contact us on the executive floor.

If you'd like to change your reservation, please give us a call.

If you need any other assistance, please call us at any time.

Let me know if there is anything else I can do for you.

Exercises

A Choose the best response to each question.

1 What does the EFL stand for?

   ⓐ excellent floor lounge

   ⓑ executive floor lounge

   ⓒ extended floor lounge

2 When are alcoholic beverages free in the EFL?

   ⓐ during happy hour

   ⓑ during breakfast hours

   ⓒ all day

3 Which department does the EFL most resemble?

   ⓐ bell desk

   ⓑ food and beverage

   ⓒ front desk

4 What information do you need to reserve an EFL meeting room?

   ⓐ a guest's age

   ⓑ a guest's room number

   ⓒ a guest's credit card number

B Match each sentence with the best reply.

1 Is my bill ready?

2 What time do you expect to check out on Monday?

3 How many people are there in your group?

4 Do you need a limousine to the airport?

5 Can you split the bill?

   ⓐ I will be checking out at 10:30 A.M.

   ⓑ That's not a problem.

   ⓒ There will be six of us.

   ⓓ Yes. Can you arrange that for me?

   ⓔ Sure. Please take a seat so that we can settle your bill.

C Complete the following conversation with the words in the box.

> free of charge   hours   place an order   refreshments   finished

Guest   Hi. I'm here to have breakfast.

Agent   I'm very sorry, sir. The breakfast [1] __________ are [2] __________ . Breakfast is from 6 A.M. to 10 A.M.

Guest   Oh, that's too bad. Maybe I should just stuff myself with some [3] __________ . They are [4] __________ , right?

Agent   Don't worry, sir. You can still have a continental breakfast by ordering room service. Would you like me to [5] __________ for you?

Guest   That sounds perfect!

A Practice checking in an executive floor guest. Take turns being a guest service agent and a guest with your partner.

> **Example**
>
> **Agent** Good morning, ma'am. How may I assist you?
>
> **Guest** I would like to check in, please.
>
> **Agent** ____

B Practice assisting an executive floor guest who wants to use the meeting room. Take turns being a guest service agent and a guest with your partner.

> **Example**
>
> **Agent** Good afternoon, sir. How may I help you?
>
> **Guest** Can I reserve a meeting room?
>
> **Agent** ____

Executive Floor Lounge (EFL)

07-05

Most of the upscale hotels located in downtown areas have an executive floor. An executive floor is also called a club floor, club lounge, business floor, or business club by hotels. Hotels designate a certain floor, usually an upper one, as the executive floor and place a private lounge on it to serve special guests. The executive floor is often described as "a hotel within a hotel." The reason is that an EFL offers almost everything that business travelers need during their stays along with a well-appointed exclusive lounge environment. These guests are mostly businessmen or VIP guests staying on the executive floor or in suites.

The executive floor lounge usually opens from 6:30 A.M. to 10:00 P.M. During the hours of operation, guests can experience private express check-in and checkout, have breakfast, and enjoy happy hour in the club lounge. In addition, they can use the meeting room next to the lounge for relaxation or meetings.

The executive floor guest service agents always stand by in the lounge so that guests can ask questions and make requests at their convenience. At some hotels, this is called butler service. This service allows executive floor guests to have their own secretaries during their stays. Since many EFL guests are repeat guests, it is very important for the EFL team to have good relationships with them and to make sure they feel comfortable.

As an EFL guest service agent, you have to be fluent in foreign languages, including English, be sociable, be well aware of global etiquette, be friendly, and always be ready to attend to the individual needs of the guests.

Words & Phrases

butler service   a special service to meet an individual guest's every need

designate   to set aside for a particular purpose

exclusive   available only to a particular group; limited to special people

relationship   a bond; a connection

repeat guest   a regular guest

secretary   a person who is employed to do office work

sociable   friendly and fond of talking to other people

upscale   designed for people who have a lot of money

well-appointed   having all the necessary furniture or equipment

08 Housekeeping

Warming Up

A Look at the picture below. Who is most likely to use this type of cart? What sort of items are inside? Share your thoughts with your partner.

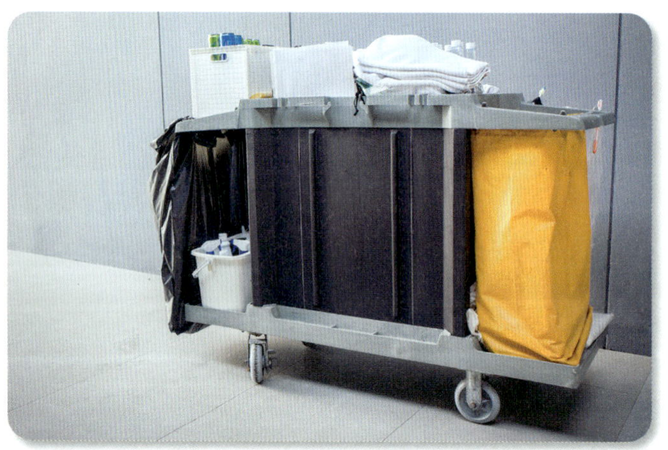

B Write the correct name for each item.

sewing kit   bandage   toilet paper   multi-adaptor

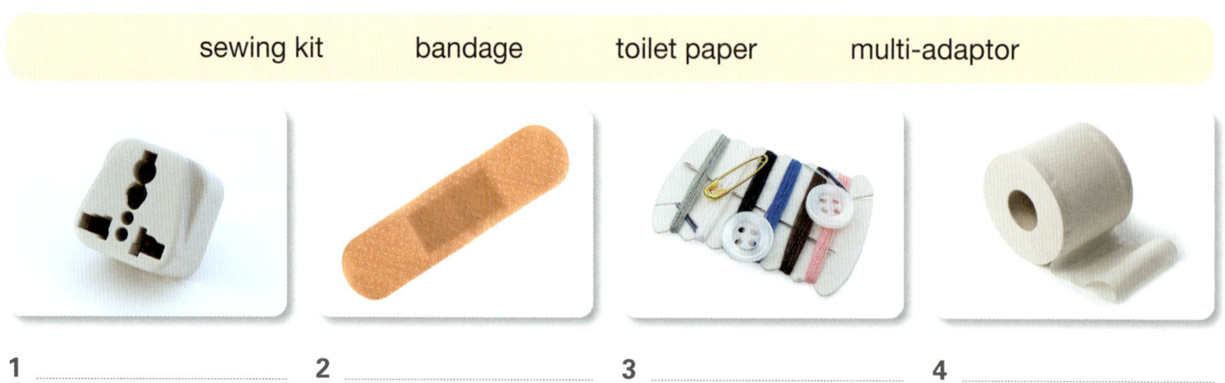

1 _____________ 2 _____________ 3 _____________ 4 _____________

  Complete each sentence with the correct word or phrase from the box.

come in	allergic to	stain	out of order	hang up	deliver

1 The air conditioner is ____________ .

2 I am ____________ feathers.

3 Housekeeping. May I ____________ ?

4 We will pick up and ____________ your laundry to your room.

5 You can ____________ the "Do Not Disturb" sign on the door.

6 Can you remove this tomato sauce ____________ from my sweater?

Hotel Terminology Learn the following words and phrases used in the hotel industry.

"Do Not Disturb" sign a sign that hotel guests can put on the door to inform the hotel staff that they don't want to be interrupted

houseman an employee who keeps guest rooms and common areas in a hotel clean and delivers amenities to guest rooms

laundry slip a paper that a guest fills out and hands in to a housekeeping staff member when requesting laundry service

make up a room to clean up a room by putting things in order and changing the linens

"Make Up Room" sign a sign that hotel guests can put on the door to inform the hotel staff that they want their rooms to be cleaned

room attendant an employee who cleans guest rooms at a hotel; a room maid

turndown service a service in which a room attendant goes into guest rooms in the early evening to tidy them up, to turn the sheets down, and sometimes to leave a mint or chocolate on a pillow prior to bedtime

 **Tips to Know**

Hotels Going Green

More and more hotels are choosing to help the environment. By doing so, they can both minimize the impact on Earth and also save hotels large amounts of water, energy, and money. There are many environmentally friendly practices that hotels carry out. For instance, some hotels put table brochures, door hangers, or pillow cards in hotel rooms to encourage their guests to reuse their towels and sheets more than once. The decision is up to the guests, but many of them are glad to participate in this kind of green campaign.

A **"Make Up Room" service**

08-01 

Attendant: Room Attendant

Attendant	Housekeeping. Hello? May I come in?[1]
Guest	Yes? What's the matter?
Attendant	May I come in to make up your room, sir?
Guest	Well… Could you come back later?[2]
Attendant	Sure, sir. I'm sorry to disturb you. Please hang up the "Do Not Disturb" sign next time. Then, you won't be disturbed, sir.
Guest	Okay, I will. Oh, can I get two face towels now?
Attendant	Sure. Here you are. When you need your room cleaned, please hang up the "Make Up Room" sign or call the operator.
Guest	Okay, thank you.
	(A few hours later…)
Attendant	Housekeeping.
Guest	Please come in.
Attendant	You hung up the "Make Up Room" sign, didn't you?
Guest	That's right.
Attendant	May I clean up your room now?
Guest	Yes, you may. How long will it take?
Attendant	It'll only take about 15 to 20 minutes, sir.
Guest	All right. Go ahead. I'll come back in 20 minutes.

Key & Alternative Expressions

1 **Housekeeping. Hello? May I come in?**

= Excuse me, sir. I'm a room attendant. Do you mind if I come in?

= Good morning, sir. It's a room maid. Can I come in?

= Room maid. Is anyone here? May I come in?

2 **Could you come back later?**

= Could you come back another time?

cf. Could you come back in another hour?
Could you come back in two hours?

B Handling "Make Up Room" service requests

🎧 08-02

Operator	Good afternoon, Ms. Daniels. How may I assist you?
Guest	Can you send someone to make up my room?
Operator	Certainly, ma'am. A maid will be there right away. Is there anything else you need?
Guest	I'd like an extra blanket. Can you also send me an iron and ironing board?
Operator	Absolutely, ma'am. I'll have a maid bring them to you.
Guest	That's so kind of you.
Operator	Thank you, Ms. Daniels.

Say the following sentences in English.

1 객실을 정비해주실 분 좀 보내주시겠습니까?

2 객실정비원이 곧 그곳으로 갈 것입니다.

3 다리미와 다리미판도 보내주시겠어요?

4 객실정비원을 시켜 가져다드리겠습니다.

5 참 친절하시군요.

Teacher's note 호텔 객실 내 타월의 종류

명칭	표준 사이즈	용도
Face Towel Washcloth	30×30 cm	• 작은 사이즈의 정사각형 타월 • 주로 손과 얼굴을 닦는데 사용하거나 샤워 중에 비누칠을 해서 몸을 닦는 용도로 사용 • 주로 욕실 세면대 근처에 비치됨
Hand Towel	40×80 cm	• 세수할 때 손과 얼굴을 닦는 용도 • 주로 욕실 세면대 근처에 비치됨 • 가정에서 흔히 사용하는 사이즈
Bath Towel	70×140 cm	• 목욕이나 샤워 후 발을 제외한 몸과 머리카락을 닦는 용도
Bath Mat	50×76 cm	• 샤워 후 발의 물기를 제거하여 미끄러움을 방지하기 위해 사용 • 주로 욕조 위나 샤워 부스 문, 손잡이 쪽에 걸어서 비치하고 사용 시에는 바닥에 깔아서 사용함

   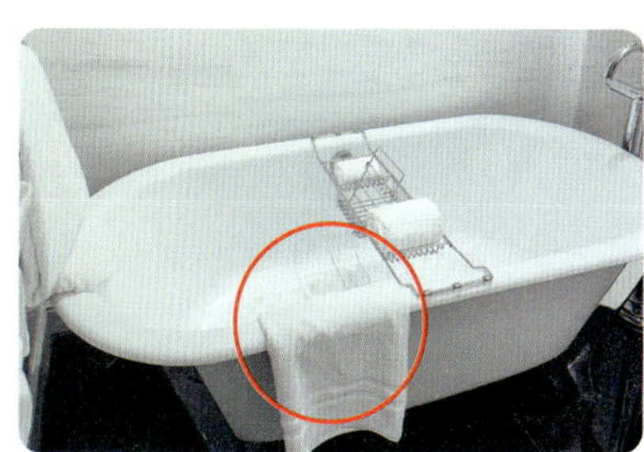

Operator	Good evening, Mr. Adams. How may I assist you?
Guest	I forgot to take off the "Do Not Disturb" sign. Can I get turndown service now?
Operator	Sure. Is there anything else you need?
Guest	Yes. Can you change my pillow? I am allergic to feathers.
Operator	Of course, sir. I will send someone with a nonallergenic foam pillow right away.
Guest	That sounds great. Oh, there is one more thing. The TV seems out of order.
Operator	I'm very sorry about that, Mr. Adams. I'll send a maintenance man to your room right away.

Say the following sentences in English.

1 깜빡하고 '방해 금지' 표지를 뗀다는 걸 잊었네요.

2 지금 객실 정돈 서비스를 받을 수 있나요?

3 저는 깃털 알레르기가 있습니다.

4 직원을 시켜 즉시 알레르기 방지 폼 베개를 올려보내겠습니다.

5 지금 바로 시설팀 직원을 객실로 보내겠습니다.

Essential Expressions   *Making Up Rooms*

1 When a guest refuses Make Up Room service

I'm sorry for disturbing you. Have a nice day.

Please forgive me for interrupting you. Have a great evening.

Please excuse me for bothering you. Have a good night.

2 Telling a guest that a request will be met

A maid will be there right away.

I'll have a maid bring them to you.

I'll send someone with a nonallergenic foam pillow right away.

I'll send a maintenance man to your room as soon as possible.

I will have it fixed immediately.

Someone will be there to fix your toilet shortly.

A Laundry service

🎧 08-04

Attendant: Laundry Attendant

Operator	Good afternoon, Ms. Carson. How may I assist you?
Guest	Hello. I have some laundry. Can you send someone to pick them up?
Operator	All right, ma'am. I will send someone up to your room right away.
	(A few minutes later…)
Attendant	Good morning, ma'am. I'm here to pick up your laundry.
Guest	Here you go. This dress needs dry cleaning.[1] There is a wine stain on a sleeve. Do you think it will come out?
Attendant	Well… We cannot guarantee it, but we will try everything to get the best results. Did you fill out the laundry slip?
Guest	Yes, I did. When can I have everything back?
Attendant	Your laundry will be delivered by noon tomorrow[2] if you use our regular service.
Guest	That late? Can you deliver it before 5 o'clock this evening? I need to wear the dress to my dinner party!
Attendant	If you are in a hurry, we have express service. You can get your laundry back within two hours, but 50% of the regular charge will be added to your bill. Is that okay?
Guest	I guess I have no choice. I'll use the express service. Charge it to my room, please.

Key & Alternative Expressions

1 This dress needs dry cleaning.

= This dress should be dry-cleaned.

cf. I'd like to have this suit pressed.
Handwash this sweater in cold water, please.
Make sure you don't use fabric softener.
This knit should be dried on a flat surface.
Please remove this chocolate stain from the shirt.

2 Your laundry will be delivered by noon tomorrow.

= Your laundry will be ready by noon tomorrow.
= We can deliver your laundry by noon tomorrow.
= We will return your laundry by noon tomorrow.

Order Taker: Housekeeping Order Taker

Caller	I stayed at your hotel a few days ago, and I believe I left something in my hotel room.
Order Taker	May I have your name and room number, please?
Caller	My name is Dora Brooks, and I don't remember my room number.
Order Taker	That's all right, Ms. Brooks. Do you remember your check-in date?
Caller	Yes. I checked in on November 12.
Order Taker	Could you tell me what you lost, please? And what does it look like?
Caller	It was my necklace. It's made of white gold, and it has a crystal pendant.
Order Taker	Let me check the list, ma'am. May I put you on hold for a moment?
Caller	Sure, go ahead.
	(A few minutes later…)
Order Taker	Hello, Ms. Brooks. You're very lucky! A maid found a necklace in your room, and we are keeping it at Housekeeping. I'm sure this is the one you lost. Do you want me to mail it to the address we have on file?
Caller	Sure. Thank you.
Order Taker	No problem. We'll charge the postage to the credit card you used when you checked out. A receipt and an invoice will be sent to your email.

Say the following sentences in English.

1 체크인 날짜를 기억하십니까?

2 어떻게 생겼습니까?

3 화이트골드로 만들어졌고, 크리스털 펜던트가 달려 있습니다.

4 객실관리부에서 보관하고 있습니다.

5 영수증과 송장은 이메일로 발송될 겁니다.

Essential Expressions   **Other Housekeeping Services**

1   Telling guests that a lost item is found

A maid found a necklace in your room, and we are keeping it at Housekeeping.

cf. I'm sorry, but we didn't find anything in your room. I will fill out a lost article report and make sure to contact you if someone finds it.

2   Asking guests about how they want a lost item back

Do you want me to mail it to the address we have on file?

Do you want it delivered? / Shall I have it delivered? / Do you want me to send it by mail?

Would you like to pick it up in person or have it delivered?

A Choose the best response to each question.

1 When a room needs to be cleaned, which sign should be put out?

   ⓐ "Make Up Room" sign

   ⓑ "Do Not Disturb" sign

   ⓒ "Please Reuse Your Towels" sign

2 Who is in charge of fixing things in guest rooms?

   ⓐ a maintenance man

   ⓑ a houseman

   ⓒ a room attendant

3 Which of the following is NOT a responsibility of Housekeeping?

   ⓐ babysitting

   ⓑ guest registration

   ⓒ handling lost & found items

4 Who picks up the guests' laundry?

   ⓐ a room maid

   ⓑ a laundry attendant

   ⓒ an order taker

B Match each sentence with the best reply.

1 May I clean this room now?

2 Is there anything else you need?

3 The heater seems to be broken.

4 When can I have my laundry back?

5 Could you tell me what you lost?

   ⓐ I'd like an extra blanket, please.

   ⓑ I'm sorry for the inconvenience.

   ⓒ Yes, you may. How long will it take?

   ⓓ It was my phone charger.

   ⓔ It will be delivered by 6 P.M.

C Complete the following conversation with the words in the box.

housekeeping	laundry	nonallergenic	disturb	make up

Room Maid   ¹____________. Hello. May I come in?

Guest   Yes, what's the matter?

Room Maid   I'm sorry to ²____________ you, but may I come in to ³____________ your room, ma'am?

Guest   Sure. Come in. Oh, by the way, can you change my pillow to a ⁴____________ foam pillow? And do you have an iron and ironing board? I have some ⁵____________ to iron.

Room Maid   Yes, ma'am. I will set them up in your room right after making up the room.

A Use the pictures below to practice handling lost & found items. Take turns being a Housekeeping order taker and a guest with your partner.

| towel | facial tissue | bathrobe | sewing kit | baby crib |

Example

Order Taker	Housekeeping. How may I help you?
Guest	Can you send me a box of facial tissues?
Order Taker	Yes, sir. I will send a box of facial tissues up to your room immediately.

B Use the pictures below to practice sending items up to a guest's room. Take turns being a Housekeeping order taker and a guest with your partner.

| watch | cell phone | necklace | earrings | passport |
| bracelet | wallet | swimsuit | laptop computer | camera |

Example

Order Taker	Housekeeping. How may I assist you?
Caller	Yes, I left a pair of earrings in my room last week.
Order Taker	Could you describe them, please?
Caller	They are ________________________

Housekeeping

Housekeeping is one of the departments in the rooms division. The primary duty of Housekeeping is to clean guest rooms, and it provides babysitting and lost and found services as well. The Housekeeping staff members often work as a team to keep every guest's room clean and attractive because the condition of the room has a strong influence on how satisfied the customer is with the hotel. Thus, the Housekeeping Department is often considered vital to a hotel.

🎧 08-06

There are different positions in Housekeeping: order takers, room attendants, room inspectors, housemen, and laundry staff members are some of them. An order taker takes phone calls from guests' rooms and handles guest requests, complaints, and lost & found items. A room attendant cleans guests' rooms and supplies them with amenities. Once a room attendant finishes her work, a room inspector checks the status of the room in terms of cleanness, facilities, and supplies.

A houseman is mainly in charge of delivering and setting up items guests request for their rooms. He carries heavy linens and towels from the maid carts. A houseman also cleans common areas such as the lobby and a meeting room in a hotel. Laundry staff members provide valet services to guests who need their clothes to be washed, dry-cleaned, or pressed. The majority of a laundry valet's job is to wash the hundreds or thousands of sheets, towels, tablecloths, and napkins that are soiled during the running of a hotel every day. Laundry staff members are also responsible for cleaning the uniforms of the hotel staff members.

📝 Words & Phrases

attractive pleasant to look at

babysitting the act of looking after children while their parents are absent

room inspector an employee who checks that everything in a guest room is in the correct condition

sheet a large piece of cloth that you sleep on or cover yourself with in a bed

soil to make dirty

status condition

supply to give someone something the person wants or needs

valet service a service that helps guests with laundry

vital very important

UNIT 09 Hotel Facilities

A Look at the picture below. Where in a hotel may you see this? Share your thoughts with your partner.

B Write the correct name for each facility in a hotel.

gym   sauna   golf driving range   swimming pool

1 _______________   2 _______________   3 _______________   4 _______________

  Complete each sentence with the correct word or phrase from the box.

overseas	copies	rent	fragile	staple	insurance

1 I have some package I want to send ________.

2 You need bubble wrap when you pack a(n) ________ item.

3 Please make five ________ of this leaflet before our meeting at 2 P.M.

4 You can make sure that your package is safely sent by purchasing shipping ________.

5 Can I ________ a baby crib for my room?

6 Please ________ these pages together.

Hotel Terminology Learn the following words and phrases used in the hotel industry.

business center   a department in a hotel that provides secretarial services, arranges meetings, does typing, sends faxes, prints and photocopies papers, and does other similar work

courier service   a service involving the sending of letters, documents, and parcels directly from one place to another

fitness center   a place where people can enjoy their leisure time by doing exercise, swimming, relaxing, or playing golf

handling charge   the cost of handling (especially the cost of packaging and mailing an order)

invoice   a list of goods or services that someone has bought; a bill

 Tips to Know

Video Conferencing System

A video conferencing system is a set of technology that enables people from multiple locations to have a conference without actually meeting in person. The system is mainly designed for online employee training sessions, web seminars, and trans-regional meetings. People can communicate simultaneously by seeing and hearing each other just like they are meeting  face to face when they use this system. They can also share data such as documents and media files in real time. Some upscale hotels that are equipped with up-to-date business facilities normally provide video conferencing systems.

A Photocopy service

09-01 

Agent: Business Center Agent

Agent Good afternoon, ma'am. How can I help you?

Guest I would like to copy these documents.

Agent Certainly, ma'am. How many copies do you need?[1]

Guest I'd like to make 5 copies of each page, please. Can you staple them as well?

Agent We can do that, but if you'd like, you can buy presentation binders. They cost 1,000 won each.

Guest Oh, that would be great. Please put the copies in the binders then.

Agent Very good, ma'am. Would you like to take a seat for a moment while I make your copies? It will take about 10 minutes.

Guest Okay. Please take your time. There is no need to hurry.[2]

(10 minutes later…)

Agent Your copies are ready, ma'am. Here you are.

Guest Great. How much do I owe you?[3]

Agent It is 25,000 won, ma'am.

Guest Can you charge them to my room account?[4] I'm in room 1615. My name is Stacy Summers.

Agent Of course, Ms. Summers. Please write your room number and sign this bill.

Key & Alternative Expressions

1 How many copies do you need?

= How many copies should I make?

2 There is no need to hurry.

= I'm not in a hurry. = I don't mind waiting. = There's no rush.

cf. Are you in a hurry [rush], sir?

3 How much do I owe you?

= How much does it cost? = How much will it cost? = How much will that be?

4 Can you charge them to my room account?

= Would you put them on my room account?

= Can you charge them to my room bill, please?

= Charge everything to my room, please.

Agent: Business Center Agent

| Agent | Good evening. Business center. Diane speaking. How may I assist you? |

Agent | Good evening. Business center. Diane speaking. How may I assist you?

Guest | Can you print some documents for me? I can't leave my room right now.

Agent | Sure. If you send us the files, we can print them and deliver them to your room. Our email address is business@sunshine.com.

Guest | That sounds perfect. I will send the files right away. How long will it take?

Agent | Your copies will be delivered within 20 minutes. Do you want me to charge the fee to your room account? Mr. McDonald, you are in room 1815, right?

Guest | Yes, that's right. Please go ahead.

Say the following sentences in English.

1 이메일로 파일을 보내주시면 저희가 출력해서 객실로 가져다드릴 수 있습니다.

2 고객님의 출력물은 20분 안에 배달될 겁니다.

C **Courier service** 🎧 09-03

Agent: Business Center Agent

Guest | Pardon me. I have something I want to send overseas.

Agent | We provide three types of international express mail services: DHL, FedEx, and EMS. Which service would you like to use?

Guest | What is EMS?

Agent | It is an express mail service provided by the Korean post office. It takes one or two days longer, but it is cheaper than DHL and FedEx.

Guest | I'm not in a hurry. I will send it by EMS.

Agent | All right. Please fill out this invoice. Is there anything fragile inside?

Guest | No, there isn't.

Agent | Would you like to purchase insurance for 10 dollars?

Guest | No, thank you.

Agent | There is a handling charge of 10,000 won. How would you like to pay it?

Guest | Put it on my room bill, please.

Say the following sentences in English.

1 이 송장을 작성해주십시오.

2 안에 깨지기 쉬운 물건이 들어 있습니까?

3 10달러짜리 보험에 가입하시겠습니까?

Agent: Business Center Agent

Agent	Good afternoon, sir. What can I do for you today?
Guest	Hello. Can I reserve a meeting room? There are eight of us.
Agent	When would you like to use the meeting room?
Guest	We need it for the entire day tomorrow starting at 9 A.M.
Agent	We have a room for eight people. The rate is 100,000 won per hour. But if you rent the room for the entire day, you only have to pay for 6 hours.
Guest	We are going to have a presentation there. What services can you provide for us?
Agent	The meeting room has free wireless Internet access and LCD TVs, and we can arrange anything you need for a presentation. You can even rent laptop computers on request.
Guest	Can we order some refreshments in the meeting room?
Agent	Of course, sir. You can order cookies and coffee or tea from room service. You can also preorder them to have them set up in the meeting room at any time you want.
Guest	Excellent! Please arrange 8 personal laptops, and coffee and cookies for eight people then.
Agent	No problem, sir. May I have your name and room number, please?
Guest	I'm Jack Morgan in room 1010.
Agent	You're all set, Mr. Morgan. We will have 8 personal laptops ready and have the kitchen prepare coffee and cookies for eight people. If you'd like to change your reservation, please give us a call.

Say the following sentences in English.

1 오늘은 무엇을 도와드릴까요?

2 회의실을 종일 대여하시면, 6시간에 해당하는 비용만 내시면 됩니다.

3 요청하시면 노트북도 대여하실 수 있습니다.

Essential Expressions   **At the Business Center**

1   **Explaining about service fees**
The meeting room rate is 100,000 won per hour.
Presentation binders cost 1,000 won each.
Printing service is free of charge up to 10 pages.
Black and white printing is 1,000 won per page.
Faxing costs vary by length and fax number.

2   **Saying that something will be ready**
We will have 8 personal laptops ready.
We will have the kitchen prepare coffee and cookies for eight people.
We will arrange a flip chart for you.

A Gym & Sauna

🎧 09-05

Agent: Fitness Center Front Desk Agent

Agent   Welcome to the fitness center. How may I assist you?

Guest   Good morning. Can I use the fitness center?

Agent   Absolutely, ma'am. May I have your room number, please?[1]

Guest   I'm staying in room 815. My name is Kelly Miller.

Agent   All right, Ms. Miller. We have a gym, indoor and outdoor swimming pools, a golf driving range, and a sauna. Which facility would you like to use today?

Guest   I'd like to work out at the gym and use the sauna.

Agent   You can use the pool and gym for free, but it costs 30,000 won to use the sauna.

Guest   That's okay. Please charge it to my room account.

Agent   Absolutely, ma'am. May I have your signature on the bill, please?[2]

Guest   Sure.

Agent   Here is your locker key for the sauna. The gym is to your left on this floor.[3] You can access the women's sauna through the gym.

Key & Alternative Expressions

1   May I have your room number, please?

= Could you please tell me your room number?

= Which room are you staying in?

= I'll need your room number.

2   May I have your signature on the bill, please?

= Can I get your signature right here, please?

= Could you sign here, please?

= Would you sign this, please?

3   The gym is to your left on this floor.

cf.   Please go through that door.

It is behind that door.

The gym is on the 1st floor.

Please go up one floor.

Please go down two floors.

Agent: Fitness Center Front Desk Agent

Guest   Is there a swimming pool at this hotel?

Agent   Yes, there is. We have both indoor and outdoor swimming pools.

Guest   How can I use them? How much are the entrance fees?

Agent   They are complimentary to hotel guests. All you need to do is tell us your room number. Then, you can get a locker key and change in the locker room.

Guest   That sounds terrific! Are kids allowed in the pools?

Agent   Of course they are. Children can use the outdoor kids' pool. If they want to use the indoor pool, a parent or guardian should be with them.

Guest   I see. What are the opening hours?

Agent   They are open from 6 A.M. to 10 P.M. Just for your information, the outdoor swimming pool is only open from June 15 to August 31.

Guest   I have my swimsuit with me, but I forgot to bring my swim cap. Can I rent one here?

Agent   Certainly, sir. The rental charge for a swim cap is 3,000 won. You can also rent goggles for the same price.

Guest   Thank you for the information. I'll come back with my kids in an hour.

Agent   My pleasure. I will see you then.

Say the following sentences in English.

1 실내 수영장과 실외 수영장이 모두 있습니다.

2 저희에게 고객님의 객실 번호만 말씀해주시면 됩니다.

3 아이들이 실내 수영장을 이용하고 싶어 하면, 부모나 보호자가 동반해야 합니다.

Essential Expressions   At the Fitness Center

1   **Telling a guest that a service is free**

It is complimentary to hotel guests.

If you are a guest of this hotel, it is complimentary [free].

There is no charge for our hotel guests.

2   **Explaining the opening hours of hotel facilities**

The pool is open from 6 A.M. to 10 P.M.

The business [opening] hours are from 6 A.M. to 10 P.M.

The operating hours are from 6 A.M. to 10 P.M.

We are open from 6 A.M. to 10 P.M.

3   **Responding to "Thank you"**

You're welcome. / My pleasure. / No problem. / Any time. / The pleasure is all mine.

A Choose the best response to each question.

1 Which service is available for guests to use at the business center?

   ⓐ photocopy service

   ⓑ body composition analysis service

   ⓒ lost & found service

2 Which of the following is NOT likely to be needed for a video conference?

   ⓐ Internet access

   ⓑ an LCD TV

   ⓒ a whiteboard

3 If guests need to send a package overseas, which department in a hotel should they contact?

   ⓐ business center

   ⓑ housekeeping

   ⓒ room service

4 What does the staff need to check before a guest uses the hotel facilities?

   ⓐ the guest's age

   ⓑ the guest's room number

   ⓒ the room rate

B Match each sentence with the best reply.

1 I would like to copy these.   •

2 They will be ready in about 10 minutes.   •

3 How long will it take?   •

4 How large is your party?   •

5 How much is the entrance fee?   •

  • ⓐ Sure. Take your time.

  • ⓑ How many copies do you need?

  • ⓒ It is complimentary to hotel guests.

  • ⓓ There are 10 of us.

  • ⓔ It will be delivered within 20 minutes.

C Complete the following conversation with the words in the box.

indoor	fitness center	facility	hours	change

Agent   Welcome to the ¹________. Which ²________ would you like to use today?

Guest   Good morning. Can I use the pool?

Agent   Of course, sir. We have both ³________ and outdoor swimming pools.

Guest   I'd like to visit the outdoor pool. What are the opening ⁴________?

Agent   It is open from 6 A.M. to 10 P.M.

Guest   Where can I ⁵________ into my swimsuit?

Agent   You can use the locker room over there.

Role-Playing

A Use the items in the pictures below to practice taking a meeting room reservation. Take turns being a business center agent and a guest with your partner.

Example

Agent Do you need anything for your meeting?

Guest Yes. We need ______________________________

B Use the information below to practice asking and answering questions about the hotel's sports facilities. Take turns being a fitness center front desk agent and a guest.

Fitness Center (3rd Floor)

- **Gym** (6:00 A.M. – 10:00 P.M.)
- **Swimming pools**
  - Indoor pool (7:00 A.M. – 10:00 P.M.)
  - Outdoor pool (10:00 A.M. – 9:00 P.M.)
- **Sauna** (6:00 A.M. – 10:00 P.M.)
- **Golf driving range** (7:00 A.M. – 10:00 P.M.)

Example

Agent Good morning. How may I help you?

Guest What kinds of sports facilities do you have?

Agent We have ______________________________

Business Center & Fitness Center

A business center at a hotel is a place that offers guests various services and equipment to help them do office work. For example, the staff members at a business center do printing, copying, photocopying, typing, faxing, and document binding for guests. In addition, secretarial services, translation and interpretation services, and courier services are available.

🎧 09-07

A business center is also usually fully equipped for business meetings and conferences. Guests can enjoy high-speed Internet connections and rent equipment such as laptop computers, beam projectors, LCD screens, flip charts, and whiteboards if they need them for their meetings. Facilities for video conferencing can be set up as well. Even office supplies such as paper clips, papers, and binders are available for purchase.

A fitness center at a hotel is a place where guests can enjoy their leisure time doing exercise, swimming, relaxing in the sauna, or playing golf. Guests can also get their body composition analyzed and measure their blood pressure or body fat.

Words & Phrases

analyze   to examine something closely

bind   to tie or fasten things together

body composition   the proportion of fat, muscle, and bone of a human body, which can be used to determine one's physical health

courier   a person who takes letters or parcels from one place to another

equipment   tools or supplies

exercise   the act of working out

flip chart   a board with large sheets of paper which can be turned over, usually used in a meeting

interpretation   translation; an explanation of what something means

measure   to find the exact size or amount of something

office supplies   materials regularly used in offices

UNIT

10 Room Service

Warming Up

A Look at the picture below. Who is the man? What is he doing? Share your thoughts with your partner.

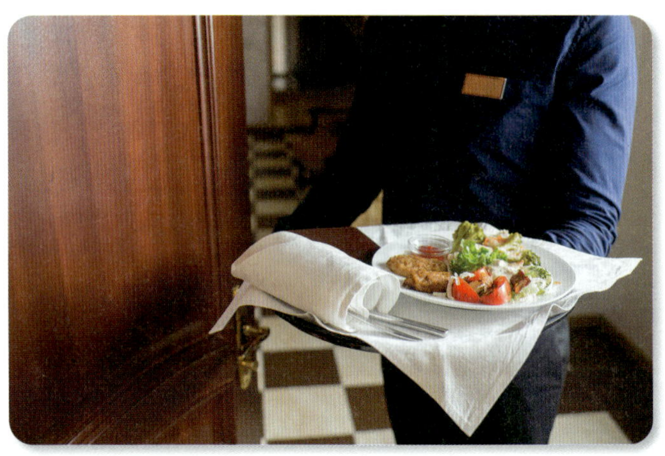

B Write the correct name for each egg dish.

scrambled eggs   fried egg [sunny side up]   omelet   boiled egg   poached egg

1 _______________   2 _______________   3 _______________   4 _______________   5 _______________

  Complete each sentence with the correct word or phrase from the box.

meal	repeat	rare	take	boiled	on the way

1 May I ________________ your order?

2 Please wait a few minutes. Your order is ________________.

3 Enjoy your ________________.

4 How do you like your eggs, fried or ________________?

5 I ordered my steak well done, but this seems too ________________ to me.

6 May I ________________ your order back to you?

Hotel Terminology Learn the following words and phrases used in the hotel industry.

doorknob service a type of service for ordering breakfast (Guests hang doorknob menus on the door handles, and then waiters collect them during the night shift.)

order slip an order pad

order taker an employee who takes a guest's order

over easy (of a fried egg) fried on both sides for a short time (Fried eggs can be cook in a variety of ways: over easy, over medium, over hard, over well.)

room service a service in which food and drinks are served in a guest's room; the people who do this work

service cart a small table with wheels used for serving food and drinks in a guest's room, usually with food warming racks

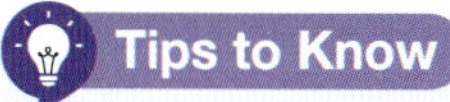 **Tips to Know**

Continental Breakfast vs. American Breakfast

Continental Breakfast
- breads: toasted bread, English muffins, bagels, biscuits, croissant, danish pastry
- beverages: coffee, tea, orange juice

American Breakfast
- breads: toasted bread, English muffins, bagels, biscuits, croissant, danish pastry
- beverages: coffee, tea, orange juice
- hot main dishes
  - eggs: fried eggs, scrambled eggs, boiled eggs, poached eggs, omelets
  - meats: ham, bacon, sausage
  - potatoes: hash browns, home fries

A Taking an order for American Breakfast

🎧 10-01 

Order Taker: Room Service Order Taker

Order Taker	Good evening. Room service. Alex speaking. How may I assist you?
Guest	Hi. I'm Theresa Perry in room 1920. How can I order breakfast for tomorrow?
Order Taker	I can take your order on the phone now, or you can fill out a breakfast order card and hang it on the doorknob.
Guest	I'd like to order on the phone now.
Order Taker	Sure. What would you like to order, Ms. Perry?
Guest	I'd like to have the American breakfast, please.
Order Taker	All right, ma'am. How would you like your eggs?
Guest	I'd like an omelet without cheese, please.[1]
Order Taker	What kind of juice would you like, ma'am?
Guest	Apple juice, and I'd like some morning pastries and a cappuccino, please.
Order Taker	What time would you like your breakfast tomorrow?[2]
Guest	Can I have it at 7:00 tomorrow morning?
Order Taker	Absolutely, ma'am. We will deliver it to your room by 7:00 A.M. tomorrow. Do you need anything else, Ms. Perry?
Guest	That's all.
Order Taker	Let me repeat your order. You ordered the American breakfast for 7:00 tomorrow morning, which includes an omelet without cheese, apple juice, morning pastries, and a cappuccino. Is it correct?
Guest	Yes, you bet!
Order Taker	Thank you for calling room service. Have a good night.

Key & Alternative Expressions

1 I'd like an omelet without cheese, please.

cf. Could I get a hamburger without onions, please?
= Please hold the onions on the hamburger.

cf. I'd like some French fries with extra ketchup, please.
= Could I have some French fries with extra ketchup?

2 What time would you like your breakfast tomorrow?
= When would you like to have your breakfast tomorrow?
= What time should we deliver your breakfast tomorrow?
= What time would you like your breakfast to be delivered [ready]?
= What time would you like to be served tomorrow?
= Do you want us to deliver it right away or at a specific time?

Order Taker: Room Service Order Taker

Order Taker	Good morning. Room service. Sharon speaking. How may I help you?
Guest	Good morning. I am in room 1004. I'd like to order the continental breakfast for two, please.
Order Taker	What kind of juice would you like, sir?
Guest	One orange juice and one grapefruit juice with a croissant, please.
Order Taker	I'm terribly sorry, but we are out of grapefruit juice. Instead of grapefruit juice, would you like to try our strawberry juice? Strawberries are in season now.
Guest	Oh, that sounds great!
Order Taker	Thank you, Mr. Wood. Do you want coffee or tea?
Guest	Coffee, please. That will be all.
Order Taker	Thank you. It will take about 15 minutes.

Say the following sentences in English.

1 어떤 주스를 드시겠습니까?

2 딸기가 요즘 제철입니다.

C **Taking an order for lunch**

Order Taker: Room Service Order Taker

Order Taker	Good afternoon. Room service. This is Miranda. How can I help you?
Guest	Hi, Miranda. This is Henry Moyer in room 1212. I'd like to order some room service, please. What is today's soup?
Order Taker	It's a tomato-based Manhattan clam chowder, sir.
Guest	Then let me have two bowls of today's soup, a club sandwich, and a cheeseburger, please.
Order Taker	How would you like your burger cooked?
Guest	Medium well done, please. Does it come with French fries?
Order Taker	Yes, it does. Do you need anything to drink?
Guest	Yes, two colas and extra ketchup on the side, please.
Order Taker	I see. Your order will be delivered within 20 minutes.

Say the following sentences in English.

1 버거는 얼마나 익혀드릴까요?

2 감자 튀김이 같이 나오나요?

3 케첩은 양을 많이 해서 따로 주세요.

🎧 10-04 

Order Taker: Room Service Order Taker

Order Taker	Good evening. Room service. Chris speaking. How may I help you?
Guest	Good evening. I would like to order dinner, please.
Order Taker	Certainly. May I have your room number, please?
Guest	It is room 630.
Order Taker	All right, Ms. Brooks. May I take your order now?
Guest	Yes. I would like to have the beef tenderloin and a glass of red wine, please.
Order Taker	How would you like your steak, ma'am?
Guest	Medium rare, please.
Order Taker	Would you like some soup or salad?
Guest	One Caesar salad, please.
Order Taker	What would you like for dessert?
Guest	Mango pudding and green tea, please.
Order Taker	Okay. Is there anything else, Ms. Brooks?
Guest	No, thank you. How long will it take?
Order Taker	I am afraid it will take more than 25 minutes since we have a lot of orders right now.
Guest	That's all right.

Say the following sentences in English.

1 수프나 샐러드 하시겠습니까?

2 디저트는 무엇으로 드릴까요?

3 죄송하지만 현재 주문량이 많아서 25분 이상 걸릴 겁니다.

Essential Expressions　Taking Orders For Room Service

1　Taking an order

What would you like to order?

What would you like to have for dinner?

2　Asking how a guest would like a steak

How would you like your steak?

How do you like your steak done [cooked]?

3　Telling a guest when room service will be delivered

It will take **about** 10 minutes.

Your order will be delivered **within** 10 minutes.

The server will be up **in** a few minutes.

We will send them up **in** about 15 minutes.

Your order will be there **in** about 20 minutes.

It will take **more than** 25 minutes because we have a lot of orders right now.

A Delivering room service

🎧 10-05

Order Taker: Room Service Order Taker / **Waiter**: Room Service Waiter

Order Taker	Good morning. Room service. This is Paul. May I help you?
Guest	I ordered my breakfast to arrive at 7:00 yesterday, but can I add one more breakfast like I ordered yesterday?
Order Taker	Are you Ms. Perry in room 1920?
Guest	Yes, that's me.
Order Taker	Please hold the line for a second. I'll check with the kitchen. (A few seconds later…)
Order Taker	Thank you for waiting. Your order is on the way.[1] Your new order will take about 10 more minutes.[2] Is that okay with you?
Guest	Excellent! Thank you.
Order Taker	You're welcome, Ms. Perry.
Waiter	Room service!
Guest	Come on in, please.[3]
Waiter	Good morning, Ms. Perry. I brought your breakfast. Where would you like to eat?
Guest	Please put everything on this table.
Waiter	All right, ma'am. Here you are. I will be back with your second order in a moment.
Guest	Thank you.
Waiter	My pleasure, Ms. Perry. Enjoy your meal.

Key & Alternative Expressions

1 Your order is on the way.
= It will be there soon.
= Your order will be up shortly.

2 Your new order will take about 10 more minutes.
= We can deliver your order in about 10 minutes.
= I will be back with your order in about 10 minutes.

3 Come on in, please.
= Please come in. The door isn't locked.

cf. One moment. I'm coming.

Waiter: Room Service Waiter

Waiter	Room service! May I come in?
Guest	Please do.
Waiter	Good afternoon, Ms. Terry. I brought the lunch you ordered.
Guest	Thank you. Could you set up a table over there, please?
Waiter	Certainly. Here you are.
Guest	Very good.
Waiter	Is there anything else you need, ma'am?
Guest	Well… I don't see my drinks. I ordered two colas.
Waiter	Oh, let me check your order slip… I'm really sorry, ma'am. The order taker must have made a mistake. I'll get your drinks immediately.
	(A few minutes later…)
Waiter	I brought your drinks, Ms. Terry. Here you are. And may I have your signature here, please?
Guest	That was fast! Sure.
Waiter	Thank you. And I apologize for the inconvenience again. I will be back to pick up the service cart in an hour. Enjoy your meal, Ms. Terry.

Say the following sentences in English.

1 저쪽에 테이블을 설치해주시겠어요?

2 주문서를 확인해보겠습니다.

3 한 시간 뒤에 서비스카트를 찾으러 오겠습니다.

Essential Expressions   Delivering Room Service

1 Acknowledging mistakes

The order taker must have made a mistake.

I'm afraid there must have been a mistake.

That is our mistake [fault].

We made an error with your order.

2 Saying that you will get something for a guest

I'll get your drinks immediately.

I'll be right back with your drinks.

I will bring your drinks right away.

3 Hoping a guest enjoys a meal

Enjoy your meal [breakfast / lunch / dinner / drink]!

Enjoy it! / Please enjoy. / Bon appetite!

Exercises

A Which items CANNOT be ordered from room service?

1 Which items CANNOT be ordered from room service?

   ⓐ an appetizer

   ⓑ an alcoholic beverage

   ⓒ a sewing kit

2 Which is NOT a type of fried egg?

   ⓐ sunny side up

   ⓑ poached

   ⓒ over easy

3 What breakfast includes egg dishes?

   ⓐ American breakfast

   ⓑ continental breakfast

   ⓒ both of them

4 Who is responsible for collecting food trays from guest rooms?

   ⓐ an order taker

   ⓑ a room service waiter

   ⓒ a room maid

B Match each sentence with the best reply.

1 I'd like to have some breakfast.

2 How would you like your eggs?

3 What time should we deliver your breakfast tomorrow?

4 How would you like your burger?

5 Would you sign here, please?

ⓐ I'd like scrambled eggs, please.

ⓑ Can I have it by 7:00 tomorrow morning?

ⓒ What would you like to order, sir?

ⓓ Sure. Here it is.

ⓔ Well-done, please.

C Complete the following conversation with the words in the box.

out of	come with	in season	bowl	medium rare

Order Taker   What would you like to order?

Guest   I'd like to order a(n) [1] _______ of broccoli soup, the sirloin steak, and a glass of red wine, please. Does the steak [2] _______ any vegetables?

Order Taker   Yes, it does. How would you like your steak?

Guest   [3] _______, please. I also want to have a glass of guava juice.

Order Taker   I'm sorry, but we are [4] _______ guava juice now. Why don't you try our tangerine juice? Tangerines are [5] _______ now.

Use the room service menu below to practice taking an order from a guest. Take turns being a room service order taker and a guest with your partner.

Room Service Menu

BREAKFAST

CONTINENTAL BREAKFAST ₩29,000
Choice of Freshly Squeezed Orange, Grapefruit, Tomato, or Apple Juice
Basket of Morning Pastries or Toast
Freshly Brewed Coffee or Tea

AMERICAN BREAKFAST ₩36,000
Choice of Freshly Squeezed Orange, Grapefruit, Tomato, or Apple Juice
Two Eggs Prepared Any Style with Bacon, Ham, or Sausage
Basket of Morning Pastries or Toast
Freshly Brewed Coffee or Tea

EGGS AND SPECIALTIES
Two Eggs Prepared Any Style with Bacon, Ham, or Sausage	₩16,000
White Omelet with Tomatoes, Asparagus, and Mushrooms	₩18,000
Freshly Baked Waffle with Strawberries and Whipped Cream	₩16,000
Buttermilk Pancakes Topped with Walnuts and Apricot Sauce	₩16,000
French Toast with Fresh Fruits and Maple Syrup	₩15,000
Fresh Fruits	₩22,000

BEVARAGES

FRESHLY SQUEEZED JUICE ₩12,000
Orange, Grapefruit, Tomato, Apple, Kiwi Juice

SOFT DRINKS ₩12,000
Cola, Diet Cola, Ginger Ale

TEA ₩12,000
Darjeeling, English Breakfast, Ceylon, Jasmine, Chamomile, Green Tea

COFFEE
Americano, Espresso	₩11,000
Café Latte, Cappuccino	₩12,000

Example

Order Taker	Taker Good morning. Room service. How may I help you?
Guest	I would like to order some breakfast, please.
Order Taker	

Room Service

One of the exclusive services that high-end upscale hotels and resorts provide is room service. Room service, or in-room dining, is a hotel service that enables guests to have their meals and drinks delivered to their rooms.

🎧 10-07

Room service is also one of the subdivisions of the Food & Beverage Department at hotel and resort properties. It usually operates on a 24-hour basis and mainly consists of three types of staff members. They are order takers, waiters, and cooks.

Order takers take guests' orders and pass them to the cooks in the kitchen. Order takers are also responsible for handling guests' complaints. Waiters deliver guests' orders to their room, set dishes up in requested places, and collect trays and carts. Waiters also take doorknob menu cards from doors during the night shift and send the guests' orders to the kitchen. Cooks prepare the food exactly the way the guests want. They often prepare food that is not on the menu for guests as long as all the ingredients are available.

📑 Words & Phrases

collect   to go and get something from the place where it is left

cook   a person whose job is to prepare food

doorknob   a round handle on a door

enable   make someone able to do something

high-end   of high quality; very expensive

ingredient   a food that you use to make a particular dish

property   a thing or building owned by someone

subdivision   a part of something which is itself a part of something larger

UNIT 11 Restaurants & Bars

Warming Up

A Look at the picture below. Where in a hotel is it? What kinds of activities can take place here? Share your thoughts with your partner.

B Write the correct job title for each hotel staff member.

waiter/waitress   greeter   busboy   bartender

1 _______________   2 _______________   3 _______________   4 _______________

  Match each word or phrase with the correct picture.

1 T-bone steak ____ **2** sirloin steak ____ **3** Caesar salad ____ **4** fried fish ____
5 sorbe ____ **6** club sandwich ____ **7** rye bread ____ **8** silverware ____

Hotel Terminology Learn the following words and phrases used in the hotel industry.

a la carte menu a menu with a separate price for each dish (↔ table d'hote)

aperitif an alcoholic drink that you have before a meals

busboy an employee who takes dirty dishes away from tables

entree the main course at restaurants or formal dinners

greeter an employee who welcomes customers politely in a restaurant

hors d'oeuvre small amounts of food that are served before the main part of a meal; an appetizer

table d'hote a complete meal consisting of a number of courses served at a fixed price with a limited choice of dishes (courses: appetizer, soup, fish, entree, salad, dessert, and beverage)

waiter/waitress an employee who serves food and drinks to diners in a restaurant

💡 **Tips to Know**

Dinner Table Etiquette at Hotel Restaurants – 5 Don'ts

1. Don't wear strong perfume. The heavy scent of it may prevent other people from enjoying the delicate aromas and flavors of their food and beverages.
2. Don't put personal belongings such as cell phones, keys, wallets, and purses on the table.
3. Don't yell or wave to get a waiter's attention. Instead, try to make eye contact with the waiter or raise your hand to call him.
4. Don't pick up a fallen piece of silverware. Just signal a waiter quietly to replace it with a new one.
5. Don't wipe your face or neck with your napkin or tuck your napkin under your chin.

A Taking a reservation

🎧 11-01 

Greeter	Good afternoon. Grace Restaurant. Ashley speaking. How may I help you?
Customer	Hello. I would like to reserve a table.[1]
Greeter	Certainly, sir. When would you like to dine here?
Customer	Tomorrow evening at seven.
Greeter	How many people are there in your party?
Customer	There will be two of us.
Greeter	What name should I make the reservation under?
Customer	Under the name of Logan Iverson.[2]
Greeter	Could you spell your last name, please?
Customer	Yes. It's I-V-E-R-S-O-N.
Greeter	All right. Can I have your contact number, please?
Customer	Sure. My number is 070-1078-7880.
Greeter	So that's a table for 2 tomorrow night at seven for Mr. Iverson. Is that correct?[3]
Customer	That's right.
Greeter	Thank you for calling, Mr. Iverson. We look forward to seeing you tomorrow.

Key & Alternative Expressions

1 I would like to reserve a table.

= I would like to make a dinner reservation.

= I'd like to book a table for two.

= Could I reserve a table (in the corner / by the window / in the nonsmoking area)?

= I need to make a reservation (for tomorrow evening).

2 Under the name of Logan Iverson.

= I made a reservation for [in the name of / under the name of] Logan Iverson.

3 So that's a table for 2 tomorrow night at seven for Mr. Iverson. Is that correct?

= This is a reservation for 2 tomorrow at 7 P.M. Is that correct?

= A table for 2 tomorrow night at seven in the name of Mr. Iverson. Is that right?

= I have reserved a table for 2 tomorrow night at seven for you. Would you like something else?

cf. May I repeat your reservation?

Let me repeat your reservation details.

Greeter	Good evening, sir. Welcome to the Universe. Do you have a reservation?
Customer	Yes, I have.
Greeter	Under what name is it, sir?
Customer	Todd Collins. I reserved a table for two.
Greeter	All right, Mr. Collins. Where would you prefer to sit?
Customer	We want a table in a quiet corner. We are having an important business meeting.
Greeter	Very well, sir. We have one in the corner. I will show you to your table. Would you come this way, please?
Customer	Thank you.
Greeter	How do you like this table?
Customer	It's great.
Greeter	Please take a seat. Here are your menus. Your waiter will be with you in a moment.

Say the following sentences in English.

1 어떤 분 성함으로 예약하셨습니까?

2 선호하시는 좌석이 있습니까?

3 구석에 자리가 하나 있습니다. 제가 테이블로 안내해드리겠습니다.

4 이쪽으로 오시겠습니까?

5 이 테이블 어떠십니까?

Greeter	Good evening. Do you have a reservation?
Customer	No, we don't.
Greeter	I'm afraid all our tables are taken. Would you mind waiting until one is free?
Customer	How long will that take?
Greeter	I am not a hundred percent sure, but I believe it will take about 10 minutes.
Customer	That's all right. We can wait.
Greeter	If you don't mind sitting separately, we can seat you very soon.
Customer	Oh, no. We want to have a table together.
Greeter	All right. Could you take a seat over there? I'll call you when a table is ready. (A few minutes later…)
Greeter	I'm very sorry to have kept you waiting. We have a table for you now. This way, please.

Say the following sentences in English.

1 죄송하지만 테이블이 다 찼습니다.

2 빈 테이블이 날 때까지 기다리셔야 하는데 괜찮으십니까?

3 저쪽 자리에 앉아주시겠습니까?

4 빈 테이블이 나면 불러드리겠습니다.

5 기다리게 해드려서 대단히 죄송합니다.

Bartender	How are you this evening?
Customer 1	Fine, thanks.
Bartender	Would you care for something to drink?
Customer 1	Sure. I will have a shot of bourbon, please.
Bartender	Would you like that straight up or on the rocks?
Customer 1	Make it a double shot on the rocks, please.
Bartender	What can I get you, ma'am?
Customer 2	Can you recommend a cocktail that isn't too sweet?
Bartender	Well, let me see… I would recommend a gin and tonic if you prefer a cocktail that isn't sweet.
Customer 2	Okay. Give me a gin and tonic with a lime in it, please.
Bartender	Certainly, ma'am.

Say the following sentences in English.

1 마실 것 좀 드릴까요?

2 스트레이트로 드릴까요, 온더록스로 드릴까요?

3 달지 않은 칵테일을 찾으시면 진토닉을 추천해드리겠습니다.

Essential Expressions — Reserving Tables & Greeting Customers

1 Asking guests if they like the table

How do you like this table?

What do you think of this table?

Will this table be fine?

Would you like this table?

2 Telling customers they have to wait

I'm afraid all our tables are taken. Would you mind waiting until one is free?

Unfortunately, we don't have any tables available at the moment. Would you mind waiting until one becomes available?

We're full at the moment. Would you mind waiting for a while?

Could you take a seat over there? I'll call you when a table is ready.

3 Suggesting an order for alcoholic beverages

Would you care for something to drink?

What can I get you (to drink)?

Can I get you something to drink?

What would you like to drink?

A Taking orders

🎧 11-05

Waiter	Good evening, ladies. Welcome to the Rose Restaurant. My name is Ryan. I'll be serving you this evening. Would you care for an aperitif before your meal?[1]
Customer 1	Yes, I'll have a glass of sherry, please.
Customer 2	Make that two, please.
Waiter	Yes, ma'am. Two glasses of sherry. Have you decided what to order?
Customer 1	No, we haven't decided yet.
Waiter	Take your time. I'll be back to take your orders with your drinks.
	(Later, the waiter comes back with the drinks.)
Waiter	Here are your drinks. May I take your order now?
Customer 1	Yes. I'd like the sirloin steak and the garden salad with Italian dressing.
Waiter	Sure. How would you like your steak?
Customer 1	Medium, please.
Waiter	All right. And you, ma'am?
Customer 2	I want to try something special from the a la carte menu. What would you recommend?
Waiter	Why don't you try our fried fish topped with crispy garlic chips, ma'am?[2] It is served with hand-cut fries and mixed salad. It's also today's special.
Customer 2	That sounds great. I'll have that. I'd like French dressing for my salad, please.
Waiter	Certainly. The fried fish and French dressing on a mixed salad. Would you like anything else, ma'am?
Customer 2	No, thank you.
Waiter	Very good. I'll be back with your dishes.

Key & Alternative Expressions

1 Would you care for an aperitif before your meal?
= Would you like a drink to start?
= Can I get you something to drink before your meal?

2 Why don't you try our fried fish topped with crispy garlic chips, ma'am?
= I'd recommend the fried fish.
= How about the fried fish?
= Have you tried the fried fish? You really should try it.

Waitress	Here you are. Enjoy your meal.
	(A few minutes later…)
Waitress	How is everything?
Customer	It's really good! Could we have a little more bread, please?
Waitress	Certainly. Is there anything else? Would you like another glass of wine?
Customer	That would be great. Could we have another round?
Waitress	Of course. I'll be right back with your bread and wine.

Say the following sentences in English.

1 식사 맛있게 하십시오.

2 식사는 어떠십니까?

3 와인 한 잔 더 하시겠습니까?

4 저희 한 잔씩 더 주시겠어요?

C **Suggesting desserts**   🎧 11-07

Waitress	I'm sorry to interrupt. May I take your plates?
Customer 1	Yes. We're finished.
Waitress	Did you enjoy your meal?
Customer 2	Everything was excellent. I especially enjoyed the sea bass.
Waitress	I'm glad you liked the food. Would you like some dessert?
Customer 1	Yes, please. Let me have the lemon sorbet and decaffeinated coffee, please.
Customer 2	I will have a slice of cheesecake and a cappuccino, please.
Waitress	Certainly. I will serve your desserts shortly.

Say the following sentences in English.

1 실례합니다.

2 접시를 치워도 되겠습니까?

3 식사는 입에 맞으셨습니까?

4 맛있게 드셨다니 다행입니다.

5 후식 좀 드시겠습니까?

Customer 1	Could we have the check, please? We would like to split the bill.
Waiter	No problem, ma'am. I'll bring separate checks. Just a moment, please.
	(A few minutes later…)
Waiter	Ladies, here are your checks.
Customer 1	Is the service charge included?
Waiter	Yes. A 10% service charge is included in the bill.
Customer 1	Can we pay here at the table?
Waiter	Of course. How will you be paying?
Customer 1	I'm going to pay with cash, and she is going to charge it to her room.
Waiter	All right, ma'am.
Customer 1	Here you are. Keep the change.
Waiter	Thank you. *(To customer 2)* Can I have your signature and room number here, please?
Customer 2	Sure. Here you are.
Waiter	It was my pleasure to serve you today. We look forward to seeing you again soon.

Say the following sentences in English.

1 계산을 따로 하고 싶은데요.

2 봉사료 10%가 계산서에 포함되어 있습니다.

3 여기에 고객님 서명과 객실 번호를 받을 수 있을까요?

Essential Expressions   **Taking Orders & Handling Payments**

1 Taking an order
Have you decided what to order? / May I take your order now? / Are you ready to order?
What would you like to order? / What would you like to have (for dinner)?

2 Offering to clean off the table
May I take your plates (away)? / May I clear away the dishes? / May I clean the table?

3 Asking about meals
Did you enjoy your meal? / How was everything? / How did you like your meal?

4 Suggesting desserts
Would you like some dessert? / Would you like to see the dessert menu?

5 Saying goodbye to diners
It was my pleasure to serve you today. We look forward to seeing you again (soon).
Thank you for dining with us. I hope you enjoyed your meal. Please come again.
Have a nice day [evening]. We hope to see you again.

Exercises

A Choose the best response to each question.

1 What do you call a type of drink that customers have before their meals?
  - ⓐ appetizer
  - ⓑ aperitif
  - ⓒ hors d'oeuvres

2 What do you call a menu that customers can choose dishes with separate prices from?
  - ⓐ a la carte menu
  - ⓑ table d'hote
  - ⓒ hors d'oeuvre

3 Who takes away dishes?
  - ⓐ a busboy
  - ⓑ a greeter
  - ⓒ a restaurant manager

4 Which is an appropriate way to call a waiter?
  - ⓐ To make eye contact with the waiter
  - ⓑ To wave at the waiter enthusiastically
  - ⓒ To yell at the waiter

B Match each sentence with the best reply.

1 Can I reserve a table for two?

2 How do you like this table?

3 Would you care for something to drink?

4 What do you recommend?

5 How would you like your check?

- ⓐ Make it separate, please.
- ⓑ Sure, I will have a whiskey on the rocks, please.
- ⓒ Why don't you try the sirloin steak?
- ⓓ It's fine.
- ⓔ Certainly, sir. For what day will that be?

C Complete the following conversation with the words in the box.

dine	taken	seat	mind	show

Greeter Good morning. Welcome to the Marina.

Customer Can we ¹_______ here now? We don't have a reservation.

Greeter I'm afraid all our tables are ²_______. Do you ³_______ waiting for 10 minutes? I will ⁴_______ you as soon as a table is ready.

(A few minites later...)

Greeter I'm very sorry to have kept you waiting. We have a table for you now. I will ⁵_______ you to the table.

Practice taking orders by using the following a la carte menu. Take turns being a waiter/waitress and a customer with your partner.

✖ Menu ✖

APPETIZERS & SOUPS

Caesar Salad	₩21,000
Chicken Salad	₩25,000
Mushroom Cream Soup	₩20,000
Seafood Soup with Garlic Toast	₩21,000

PASTAS & SANDWICHES

Seafood Spaghetti with Tomato Sauce or Cream Sauce	₩29,000
Bolognese Spaghetti	₩27,000
Hamburger	₩29,000
Cheeseburger (Choice of Cheddar, Gruyere, or Brie Cheese)	₩33,000
Club Sandwich	₩27,000

GRILL

Beef Tenderloin	₩49,000
Ribeye	₩53,000

DESSERTS

Mango Pudding	₩14,000
Ice Cream (Vanilla, Strawberry, Chocolate)	₩12,000
Sherbet (Mango, Raspberry, Yoghurt)	₩12,000

BEVERAGES

FRESHLY SQUEEZED JUICE

Orange, Grapefruit, Tomato, Apple, Kiwi	₩12,000

SOFT DRINKS

Cola, Diet Cola, Sprite	₩12,000

TEA

Darjeeling, English Breakfast, Ceylon, Jasmine, Chamomile, Green Tea	₩12,000

COFFEE

Americano, Espresso	₩11,000
Café Latte, Cappuccino	₩12,000

Example

Waiter	Good afternoon, sir. May I take your order?
Customer	I would like a hamburger, please.
Waiter	

Restaurants

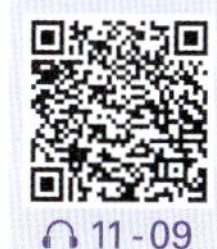

🎧 11-09

Most full service hotels & resorts have several fine dining restaurants. Fine dining restaurants offer special services with specific dedicated meal courses. The interiors of these restaurants are of high quality, and they are also very spacious. The wait staff is highly trained and often wears formal attire. These hotel restaurants have certain dining rules that people are generally expected to follow, often including a dress code.

There are three main reasons why diners choose to eat at a hotel restaurant despite its very expensive prices: the atmosphere, service, and menu. Hotel restaurants try their best to keep their atmosphere relaxing and pleasant by taking many factors into consideration, such as the layout of the tables, the lighting, and the music. They try to put enough space between each table to allow customers to have some privacy. The restaurants don't make the lights too bright for diners. They keep the volume of the music low in order not to disturb customers. Some hotel restaurants even decide not to have any music at all for fear that it will overpower the dining space.

The wait staff is as important as the elements above. The service that the wait staff provides goes far beyond taking orders from customers and delivering food to tables. Waiters look for signals from customers, anticipate what kind of service individuals want, and then give personalized service to each customer. Waiters also need to have professional knowledge about all the food served. They should be able to answer all questions customers have about the menu or wine. They should also be ready to make menu recommendations if asked.

📝 Words & Phrases

atmosphere   the mood or feeling that a place has; ambience

attire   the clothes a person is wearing

dedicated   devoted; wholehearted

diner   someone who is eating a meal in a restaurant

dress code   a set of rules about what people should wear in a particular place

layout   the way that something is arranged

lighting   equipment for producing light

overpower   to spoil something by having much stronger power

personalized   designed to be suitable for a particular person

take into consideration   to think about a particular thing when making a decision

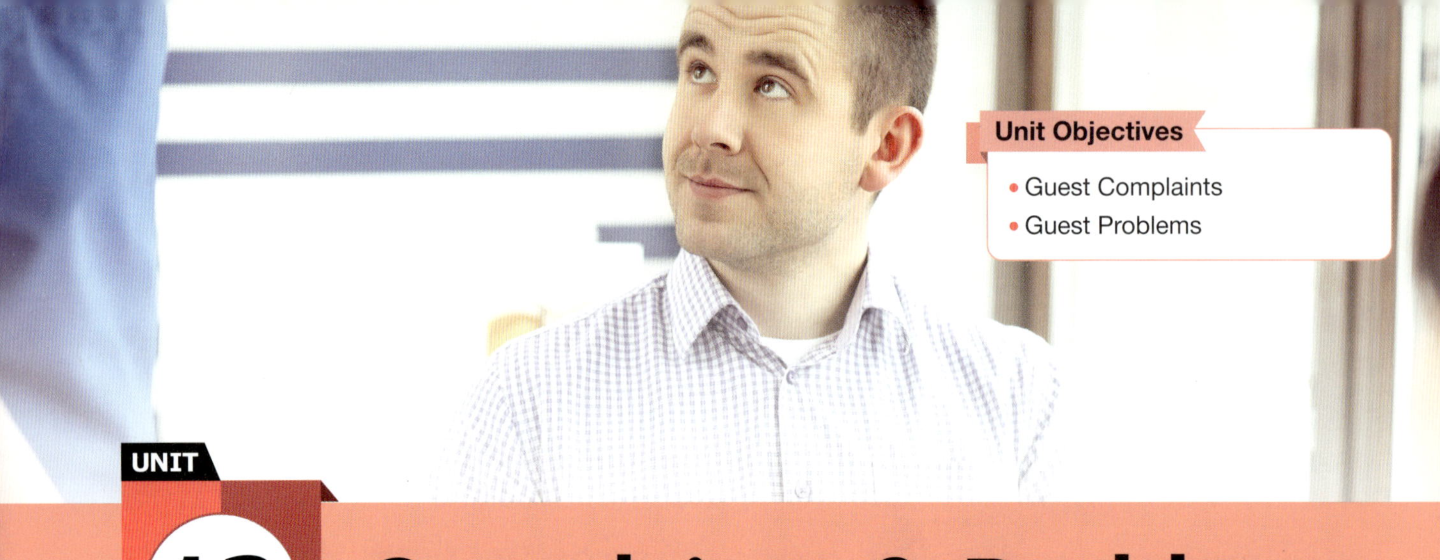

12 Complaints & Problems

Warming Up

A Look at the picture below. What seems to be the problem? Share your thoughts with your partner.

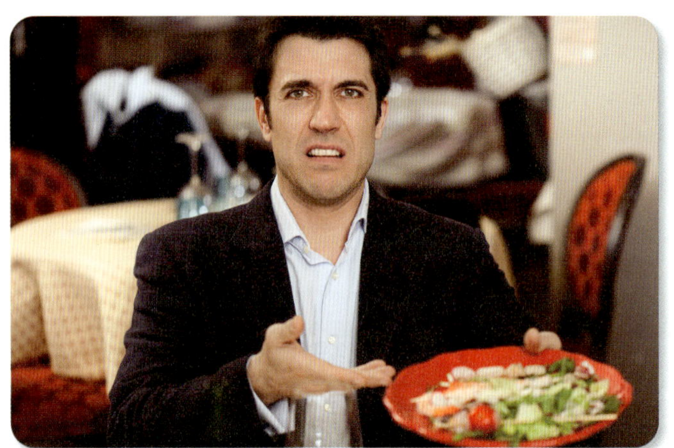

B What should hotel staff members say to guests with complaints? Check the correct boxes.

ⓐ I'm very sorry for the inconvenience. ☐	ⓑ Please accept my apology. ☐
ⓒ I've been working hard. ☐	ⓓ Please give me a gratuity for my sincere service. ☐
ⓔ This is someone else's fault. ☐	ⓕ Please forgive us for the mistake. ☐
ⓖ I'm very sorry. Could you tell me what exactly happened, please? ☐	ⓗ I'm terribly sorry, but these things happen. ☐

 Match each word or phrase with its correct definition.

1 report	ⓐ to take off; to remove
2 upgrade	ⓑ to give someone a better room in a hotel
3 manager	ⓒ to accidentally let a liquid flow out of its container
4 deduct	ⓓ to tell someone that something has happened
5 replace	ⓔ a feeling of comfort that someone gets when something unpleasant has not happen
6 spill	ⓕ to leave a place for a short amount of time
7 overcook	ⓖ to make water go through a toilet by pressing a handle
8 relief	ⓗ to cook food for too long
9 flush	ⓘ an employee who is in charge of a department
10 clog	ⓙ to block something so that nothing can pass through

Hotel Terminology   Learn the following words and phrases used in the hotel industry.

chef   a professional cook who works in a hotel, especially the main cook

complimentary   free; courtesy; on the house

safety deposit box   a strong metal box with a lock in which people can keep their money or valuable things, usually located in a guest room or at the front desk in a hotel

welcome card   a paper card that is put in guest rooms to convey a message that a hotel welcomes their guests

Tips to Know

Employee Empowerment

Employee empowerment means giving frontline employees more freedom, flexibility, and power to make decisions on the spot without asking their superiors. In the hotel industry, employee empowerment is especially important because it provides some practical advantages to a hotel. First, customer satisfaction will increase since empowered workers can respond to guests'  problems and complaints more quickly and flexibly. Second, employee satisfaction will also improve. Studies show that empowered staff members tend to feel more motivated and involved in their work. The reason is that they take personal pride in providing guests with high-quality services on their own, thus contributing to their company.

A Complaints about room facilities

🎧 12-01

Manager: Front Desk Manager

Receptionist	Good evening. Front desk. Ted speaking. How may I help you?
Guest	I just checked into room 707, but there is a problem with it.
Receptionist	What exactly is the problem?
Guest	There's no hot water coming out.[1]
Receptionist	I'm sorry, Ms. Murphy. I'll send someone up immediately.
	(1 hour later…)
Guest	Hello. May I speak to Ted?
Receptionist	Speaking. How can I help you?
Guest	I asked you to send someone up about an hour ago, but no one has showed up yet. It's been a long day, and I desperately need a hot shower. I really need you to do something about it right now.
Receptionist	I'm terribly sorry for the inconvenience, Ms. Murphy. I will have the repairman rush there now.
Guest	No, no. I can't just sit here and wait another hour for someone to appear. I want you to change my room.
Receptionist	I'm sorry, but we have a full house today, ma'am. There is nothing I can do about it.
Guest	Can I speak to the manager?
Receptionist	Sure. One moment, please.
Manager	This is the front desk manager, Dewey Carson. I heard you are not happy with our service. I sincerely apologize for the unpleasant experience you just had.
Guest	I never expected such bad service at your hotel. The room has a couple of major issues, and your receptionist was being so stiff and totally lacks flexibility. I'm really disappointed.
Manager	I understand, ma'am.[2] Again, I'm very sorry for the oversight. I've upgraded your room to a suite. I'll send up a bellman with a new key right away. I assure you that it won't happen again.[3]

1 There is no hot water coming out.

> **cf.** The safety deposit box is not working.
> The TV is broken.
> The light bulb has burned out.
> The electric kettle won't turn on.
> The alarm clock radio is malfunctioning.
> Something has gone wrong with the hair dryer.

2 I understand, ma'am.

= I can imagine how frustrating it must have been.

= I realize this matter is very important to you.

= I know the incident must have been very unpleasant for you.

3 I assure you that it won't happen again.

= I will make sure this won't happen again.

= We will take steps to ensure this will never happen again.

= I give you my word this won't happen again.

= You have my word this will not happen again.

= Please rest assured that such a thing will not happen again.

Teacher's note 사람의 성향을 나타내는 단어

구분		형용사	뜻	뉘앙스
긍정적		kind, empathetic, thoughtful	친절한, 공감하는, 사려 깊은	남을 배려하고 이해하는 태도
		confident, optimistic, brave	자신감 있는, 낙관적인, 용감한	자기 확신과 긍정적 태도
		humble, generous, reliable	겸손한, 관대한, 신뢰할 수 있는	겸손하며 남을 돌보고 믿음을 주는
		diligent, hardworking	성실한, 근면한	꾸준히 노력하는 태도
부정적		stubborn, rigid, stiff	고집 센, 딱딱한, 경직된	융통성 없고 유연하지 않은 태도
		selfish, rude, arrogant	이기적인, 무례한, 거만한	남을 배려하지 않고 불쾌한 태도
		lazy, careless, thoughtless	게으른, 부주의한, 생각 없는	책임감 부족하거나 신중하지 않은 행동
중립적/기타		outgoing, extroverted, introverted	사교적인, 외향적인, 내향적인	사회적 성향의 유형
		impulsive, spontaneous	충동적인, 즉흥적인	계획적이지 않고 순간에 따라 달리 행동하는

Cashier	Here is your bill. Please check it over to see if there is anything wrong, Mr. White.
Guest	This isn't right. There is a minibar charge here, but I didn't use it at all.
Cashier	Let me check on the detailed bill, sir. You were charged for five cans of soft drinks.
Guest	I just took them out of the fridge to make room for my mineral water.
Cashier	Now I see. The minibar staff member probably thought you drank them all. I'm sorry for the inconvenience. I will deduct them from your bill now.

Say the following sentences in English.

1 잘못된 것이 있는지 확인해주십시오.

2 세부 계산서를 확인해보겠습니다.

3 불편을 끼쳐서 죄송합니다.

4 계산서에서 그것들을 지금 제해드리겠습니다.

C Complaints about the wrong room 🎧 12-03

Receptionist	Front desk. Thank you for calling. This is Dustin speaking. What can I do for you?
Guest	I just checked into room 1012. But I don't think this is my room. There are a basket of fruit and a bottle of wine on the table. I wish those were mine, but someone else's name is written on the welcome card. My name is Cindy Collins, but the name on the card is Gerald Pearson.
Receptionist	I'm really sorry for what happened, ma'am. I am afraid there must have been a mistake.
Guest	That's all right. I was just a little surprised. So what should I do now?
Receptionist	I will give you a new room. Please stay in the room until our bellman comes up to your room. As a token of our apology, allow us to give you a complimentary bottle of wine.

Say the following sentences in English.

1 죄송하지만 착오가 있었던 것 같습니다.

2 사과의 표시로 저희가 무료 와인 한 병을 드리게 해주십시오.

D Complaints about restaurant service

🎧 12-04

Guest Excuse me. We have some problems with our meals.

Waiter What seems to be the problem, ma'am?

Guest I ordered my steak medium well done, but this steak is overcooked. In fact, it's basically burned!

Waiter I'm terribly sorry that your steak is not cooked as you requested. I'll take it back to the kitchen and have the chef cook a new one. It will be ready in about 15 minutes. Are there any other problems, ma'am?

Guest Yes, there is. My husband hasn't gotten his sandwich yet. Why is it taking so long?

Waiter I'm really sorry, ma'am. I will check on his order with the kitchen.

Guest Thanks. Oh, one more thing. Can you change my cup? It has a lipstick stain on the rim.

Waiter I'm terribly sorry, ma'am. I will replace it with a clean one right away.

(After the meal…)

Waiter Here are some desserts for you. They are on the house.

> **Say the following sentences in English.**

1 어떤 문제가 있습니까?

2 저는 스테이크를 미디엄 웰던으로 주문했는데, 이 스테이크는 너무 익었어요.

3 고객님의 스테이크가 요청하신 대로 조리되지 않아 대단히 죄송합니다.

4 주방으로 다시 가져가서 주방장에게 새로 요리해달라고 하겠습니다.

5 한 15분이면 준비될 겁니다.

6 혹시 다른 문제도 있습니까?

7 주방에 주문 상태를 확인해보겠습니다.

8 가장자리에 립스틱 자국이 있어요.

9 깨끗한 컵으로 즉시 교체해드리겠습니다.

10 여기 디저트입니다. 서비스로 드리는 겁니다.

1 Apologizing to guests

I'm very [extremely / awfully / terribly] sorry for the inconvenience.

I apologize for the mistake [error].

I sincerely apologize for the experience you just had.

I'm really sorry for what happened.

I'm terribly sorry about the delay [accident / mix-up].

Please accept my apology.

2 Giving solutions to poor service

I've upgraded your room to a suite.

I will give you a new room.

I will deduct [remove] that charge from your bill.

Allow us to give you a complimentary bottle of wine.

Let me make it up to you with a complimentary bottle of champagne.

I'll take it back to the kitchen and have the chef cook it properly.

I'll bring you a new one.

I'll replace it with a new one.

I'd like to offer you a 50% discount voucher for your next stay.

Conversation **Ⅱ** Guest Problems

A Guest mistakes

🎧 12-05

Operator	Good evening, Ms. Wright. How may I assist you?
Guest	There are some problems in my room. My kids spilled juice all over the bed.[1] In addition, they knocked a coffee cup off the table and broke it. Can you send someone to change the sheets and to clean up the broken pieces?
Operator	Oh, did anyone get hurt?
Guest	Fortunately, we are fine, but it is a complete mess in here.
Operator	What a relief! I will report the problems to Housekeeping and have them send a room attendant up immediately.
Guest	Thank you so much.
Operator	My pleasure, Ms. Wright. If you need anything else, just give us a call.

Key & Alternative Expressions

1 My kids spilled juice all over the bed.

= My kids dropped a glass and spilled juice on the bed.

cf. Most common complaints from hotel guests

Housekeeping

The toilet won't flush.

The water keeps running in the toilet.

I can't turn off the faucet.

The sink is stopped up [blocked / plugged up].

The plughole in our sink is clogged up with hair.

There isn't any soap in the bathroom.

The air conditioner in my room doesn't work.

I'm allergic to feather pillows.

The TV is out of order.

A staff member ignored the "Do Not Disturb" sign.

The room smells of smoke.

Laundry

There is still a stain on my shirt.

My scarf is faded.

My blouse is missing. It was never returned.

Front Desk

The room is too small.

This isn't the type of room I reserved.

This isn't my bill.

I've been overcharged on my bill.

There is a lot noise coming from the room next door.

A staff member was impolite.

Restaurant

This meal isn't warm enough.

This salad is too salty.

The silverware is stained.

My steak is overcooked.

The food was spilled while it was being served.

The wait staff member was inattentive.

Operator	Good evening, Mr. Norman. How may I assist you?
Guest	Are you heating my room? It's too hot in here, and I can't lower the temperature.
Operator	Could you check the control box? Please press the "OFF" button in the cooling & heating section on the control panel.
Guest	I already did that, but it made no difference.
Operator	In that case, how about turning on the air conditioner?
Guest	Where is the remote control? I can't find it.
Operator	Have you checked on the bedside table?
Guest	Yes, I did. But there was only one for TV.
Operator	You use that for everything in the room. You'll find buttons for the air conditioner at the bottom of it.
Guest	Ah, there it is. Thank you.

Say the following sentences in English.

1 객실에 지금 난방이 가동 중인가요?

2 객실 안이 너무 더운데 온도를 낮출 수가 없어요.

3 (냉난방) 조절기를 확인해보시겠습니까?

4 침대 옆 탁자도 확인해보셨습니까?

5 그것을 사용해 객실 내 모든 것을 제어할 수 있습니다.

Essential Expressions   **Guest Problems**

1   Asking guests to check something

Could you check the control box?

Could you try turning it off and on again?

Could you check if the power is on?

2   Giving solutions to problems with rooms

I will report the problems to Housekeeping.

I'll contact Maintenance immediately.

I'll send someone from Maintenance to fix it.

I'll send up a room attendant as soon as possible.

We can change your room to another one.

I'll have a room attendant change the sheets right away.

I will supply it immediately.

Exercises

A Choose the best response to each question.

1 Who is responsible for fixing the facilities in guest rooms?

    ⓐ a houseman

    ⓑ a maintenance person

    ⓒ a room attendant

2 Which problem is the front desk NOT in charge of handling?

    ⓐ A nonsmoking room smells like smoke.

    ⓑ A room is too small.

    ⓒ The sink in the bathroom is stopped up.

3 Who delivers the new key to a guest who will change rooms?

    ⓐ a bellman

    ⓑ a doorman

    ⓒ a houseman

4 If a guest room strongly smells like smoke, what most likely will the hotel staff do?

    ⓐ try airing out the room

    ⓑ contact Maintenance immediately

    ⓒ move the guest to another room

B Match each sentence with the best reply.

1 There are some problems in my room.

2 I didn't expect such bad service in here.

3 Here is your bill. Please look it over.

4 Did anyone get hurt?

5 You should press the "OFF" button.

  ⓐ We are terribly sorry for the inconvenience.

  ⓑ I already did.

  ⓒ Fortunately, no one got hurt.

  ⓓ What exactly are the problems?

  ⓔ This isn't right.

C Complete the following conversation with the words in the box.

burned	apologize	ready	token	replaced

Guest Excuse me. When will my burger be [1] __________?

Waiter I'm sorry that it is taking a while. I will check with the kitchen… Here you are. Enjoy your lunch.

Guest Wait! The patty is just [2] __________!

Waiter I [3] __________ on behalf of the kitchen. I will talk to the chef and have it [4] __________ immediately.

Waiter Here is your hamburger. Please accept this bottle of champagne as a [5] __________ of our apology.

Make your own complaints by using each picture and practice handling them with your partner. Take turns being a hotel staff member and a guest with your partner.

Example

| Receptionist | Good evening. Front desk. How may I help you? |
| Guest | |

Example

| Operator | Good afternoon, ma'am. What can I do for you? |
| Guest | |

Example

| Waitress | How is your meal, sir? |
| Guest | |

Handling Complaints

No matter how hard the hotel staff tries to provide quality service for guests, it is hard to avoid customer complaints. Although no one likes receiving complaints, they give the staff members an opportunity to identify problems with their service. Complaints can also help create a bond between the staff and the customers, which can lead to customer loyalty.

🎧 12-07

There are key five steps to handling complaints properly. First, **LISTEN** carefully to a guest with an open mind. Take time to listen to what the person has to say without prejudging the situation. Maintain eye contact and let the person say everything about his or her concern. Second, **EMPATHIZE**. When listening to a complaint, try to understand how the guest feels. Put yourself in the guest's shoes, but do not make any excuses or blame others. Third, **APOLOGIZE** even if you think you have no part in the situation and you are sure that something will be done to remedy the issue. A sincere apology after a service failure can regain goodwill. Fourth, **TAKE ACTION PROMPTLY**. Try to solve a guest's problem with his or her suggested solution or an alternative you can provide as quickly as you can. In some cases, you may even need to provide a small gift to the guest to compensate him or her for the inconvenience and to thank the guest for giving you the chance to improve your service. Fifth, **FOLLOW UP**. Once you have gone through the previous steps, call the guest a week later to find out if he or she is satisfied with the solution.

📝 Words & Phrases

blame   to say that someone is responsible for a bad situation

bond   a close relationship between people

compensate for   to make up for

empathize   to understand someone else's feelings or problems

goodwill   a kind and friendly attitude toward someone or something

have no part in   not to be involved in something

identify   to find out what something is

prejudge   to judge a situation before having enough information

put oneself in one's shoes   to imagine how someone else feels in a situation

regain   to get something again

remedy   to correct or improve a situation

Answer Key

01 Switchboard

Warming Up
p.8

B

ⓐ ☑ ⓑ ☑
ⓒ ☐ ⓓ ☑
ⓔ ☐ ⓕ ☑
ⓖ ☑ ⓗ ☐

Vocabulary
p.9

1 ⓓ   2 ⓐ
3 ⓔ   4 ⓒ
5 ⓗ   6 ⓕ
7 ⓖ   8 ⓑ

Conversation ❶

Giving Information
p.10

B Giving information about hotel facilities

1 Thank you for calling the Lunar Hotel.
2 Does your hotel have a swimming pool?
3 The pool is located on the 5th floor inside the fitness club.
4 The pool is open from 7 A.M. until 10 P.M.

C Giving information about hotel services I

1 How may I help you?
2 It's 15,000 won to watch one movie and 20,000 won to watch movies all day.
3 Is there anything else I can help you with?

D Giving information about hotel services II

1 You can have breakfast at the cafe in the lobby.
2 The breakfast buffet is served from 5 A.M. to 10 A.M.
3 Room service is available 24 hours a day.

Conversation ❷

Handling Guest Requests
p.13

B Connecting a guest's call to an employee in a hotel department

1 May I ask who is calling, please?
2 I'm sorry, but the line is busy.
3 Would you like to leave a message?
4 I'm afraid Mr. Lee just stepped out of the office.
5 He will probably be back by three.
6 Shall I have him call you when he returns to the office?

C Wakeup call service

1 Good evening. Tiffany speaking. What can I do for you?
2 Could you give me a wakeup call at six tomorrow morning?
3 Good morning, Mr. Brown. This is your 6 A.M. wakeup call.
4 Have a great day.

D Handling a wrong number

1 Mr. Chung is not a guest at this hotel.
2 I'm sorry, but there is no one here by that name.
3 What number are you calling?
4 I'm afraid you called the wrong hotel.

Exercises
p.17

A

1 ⓐ   2 ⓑ
3 ⓑ   4 ⓒ

B

1 ⓐ   2 ⓔ
3 ⓓ   4 ⓑ
5 ⓒ

C

1 speaking
2 assist
3 connect
4 busy
5 hold

02 Reservations

Warming Up
p.20

B

ⓓ

Vocabulary
p.21

1 on behalf of
2 book
3 arrange
4 extra
5 guarantee
6 available

Conversation ❶

Taking Room Reservations
p.22

B Explaining a cancelation policy

1 Are there any rooms available?
2 How many nights will you be staying?
3 The rate is $250 per night, including tax and service charges.
4 What is your cancelation policy?

C Putting a customer on the waiting list

1 I'm trying to reserve a room for this weekend.
2 I'm awfully sorry, but we have no rooms available for this weekend.
3 Shall I give you the number of another hotel nearby?
4 Can you just put me on the waiting list?

D Taking an executive floor (EFL) room reservation

1 Do you have any rooms available on the executive floor?
2 It's nice to have you back, Mr. Lee.
3 Would you like to use the same credit card on file?
4 Could you give me the credit card number to guarantee the reservation?
5 You're all set.
6 Please let me know your flight number and your time of arrival.

E Handling special requests

1 How many are you in your family?
2 How old are your kids?
3 There is a $30 charge for an extra bed.

Conversation ❷

Handling Requests After Reservations
p.26

B Changing reservations

1 I'd like to change my reservation, please.
2 Let me check on that.
3 You have a reservation for a deluxe twin room for 3 nights starting on May 23.
4 I've changed that for you.

C Canceling reservations

1 I'd like to cancel a reservation, please.
2 I'm calling on behalf of Mr. David Johns.
3 Excuse me, but may I ask who is calling?
4 I've canceled his reservation.

Exercises
p.29

A

1 ⓒ   2 ⓐ
3 ⓐ   4 ⓑ

B

1 ⓔ   2 ⓐ
3 ⓒ   4 ⓑ
5 ⓓ

C

1 vacancies
2 arriving
3 staying
4 offer
5 including

03 Door & Bell Desk

Warming Up p.32

B

ⓑ

Vocabulary p.33

1 revolving door
2 inconvenience
3 unload
4 escort
5 spacious
6 shelf

Conversation ❶

Doorman Service p.34

C Valet parking services I

1 Where should I park my car?
2 Just leave your car here.
3 I will have someone take care of everything.

D Valet parking services II

1 Could you get my car, please?
2 What's the plate number?
3 I'll bring your car immediately.

E Saying farewell to a guest

1 Are you leaving now?
2 Did you enjoy your stay with us?
3 I'm pleased to hear that.
4 Do you need a taxi?
5 Here comes a taxi.
6 I'll put your luggage in the trunk.

Conversation ❷

Bellman Service p.37

B Showing a guest his or her room

1 Let me show you your room.

2 You'll get charged for what you use when you check out.
3 There are two bottles of complimentary mineral water on the shelf.
4 Our hotel has a no-tipping policy.
5 A service charge will be added to your final bill.

C Baggage down service

1 Can you send a bellman to my room?
2 I'm checking out in 10 minutes.
3 How many bags do you have?
4 I have two suitcases and one carry-on bag.
5 I will send someone up immediately.

D Holding baggage

1 Can my husband and I leave our bags at the hotel?
2 Let me store your luggage in our checkroom until you come back.
3 Can I have your name and room number?
4 Are these your only bags?
5 Here is your baggage claim tag.

E Handling complaints about baggage delivery

1 I've been waiting for my bags to be sent up for almost 30 minutes!
2 I'm terribly sorry for the delay, Ms. Baker.
3 I'll check on that right away and get back to you.
4 Your bags are on the way now.
5 I'm very sorry for the inconvenience.

Exercises p.41

A

1 ⓒ	2 ⓑ
3 ⓑ	4 ⓒ

B

1 ⓑ	2 ⓔ
3 ⓒ	4 ⓓ
5 ⓐ	

C

1 way
2 After
3 get

4   complimentary

5   charged

04 Front Desk I (Reception)

Warming Up   p.44

B

ⓐ

Vocabulary   p.45

1   fill out

2   lock out

3   imprint

4   extend

5   get through

6   set

7   inventory

8   closet

Conversation ❶

Check-In Service   p.46

B Check-in process II

1   May I have your business card for registration?

2   Could you fill out this registration form?

3   May I have your credit card to make an imprint?

4   The bellman will take you up to your room.

5   If you have any questions, press 0 on the room phone.

C Checking in walk-in guests

1   Do you have a room available for tonight?

2   We can offer you that room at a rate of $280 a night plus tax and service charge.

D Checking in guests with reservation problems

1   I'm very sorry, but we don't have a reservation under that name.

2   Do you have a confirmation number?

3   I will check you in now, and I will confirm your reservation as soon as the Reservation Department opens tomorrow.

Conversation ❷

In-House Guest Service   p.49

B Guest inquiries about a hotel shuttle service

1   Do you provide a shuttle service for hotel guests to the downtown area?

2   We operate a courtesy shuttle bus between the hotel and downtown every hour.

3   The last shuttle bus leaves from the hotel at 9 P.M.

C Assisting a locked-out guest

1   I'm locked out of my room.

2   Could I see some picture ID, please?

D Guest inquiries about hotel facilities

1   The pool and the gym are complimentary for all of our hotel guests.

2   Where can I have breakfast?

3   The cafe serves breakfast from 5:30 A.M. to 10:00 A.M.

4   Is breakfast included in the price?

5   Your package includes a daily breakfast for two.

E Extending a stay & providing an extra bed

1   Can I extend my stay for another night?

2   Let me check if the room is available.

3   I extended your stay one more night.

4   Can I request an extra bed in my room?

5   We can set one up for the additional charge of $20 per night.

Exercises   p.53

Ⓐ

1 ⓐ	2 ⓐ
3 ⓐ	4 ⓒ

Ⓑ

1 ⓔ	2 ⓑ
3 ⓐ	4 ⓒ
5 ⓓ	

C

1 confirmation

2 booked

3 overlooking

4 choice

5 imprint

UNIT

05 Front Desk II (Cashier)

Warming Up p.56

B

1 credit card

2 traveler's check

3 bills

4 coins

Vocabulary p.57

1 bill

2 look it over

3 remove

4 exchange

5 mistake

6 settle

Conversation ❶

Checkout Service p.58

B Checking out a guest

1 Let me help you with that.

2 What room were you in?

3 How was your stay with us?

4 Did you use the minibar since last night?

5 It looks like you had breakfast at the cafe this morning.

6 Your total is 350,000 won.

7 Please look it over to see if everything is accurate.

C Settling a bill

1 Are you using the same credit card you gave me when you checked in?

2 Can I pay with cash?

3 Your total comes to 220,000 won.

4 How much is that in U.S. dollars?

5 Here is your change. It's 20,000 won.

D Extending the checkout

1 Let me check if the room is available first.

2 You can stay in your room until 6 P.M., but will be charged 50% of the room rate.

3 If I check out before noon, can I leave my luggage somewhere in the hotel?

4 If you need some more time to pack your luggage, I can extend your checkout around 30 minutes at no extra charge.

Conversation ❷

Handling Disputed Charges & Other Cashiering Services p.62

B Settling an account with a credit card

1 Please check it over to make sure everything is correct.

2 How would you like to pay?

3 I'm sorry, but your card was declined. Do you have another one?

C Exchanging money

1 Today's exchange rate is 1,100 won to the dollar.

2 How much would you like to change?

3 How would you like your bills?

D Handling guest complaints during checkout

1 Are you leaving one day earlier than expected?

2 Your room charge will be put on your company account.

3 Here is your itemized bill for the incidental charges.

4 I'll put a note in your profile.

5 I assure you it won't happen again on your next visit.

Exercises p.65

A

1 c   2 a
3 a   4 c

B

1 c   2 a
3 d   4 b
5 e

C

1 prepare
2 number
3 check
4 paying
5 staying

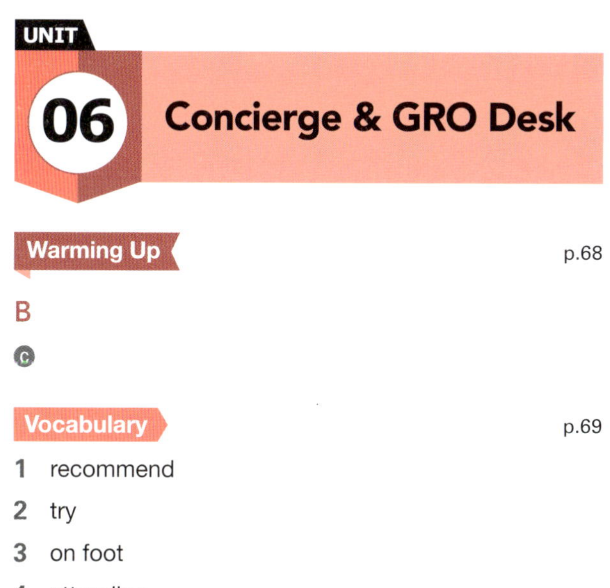

UNIT 06 Concierge & GRO Desk

Warming Up p.68

B
c

Vocabulary p.69

1 recommend
2 try
3 on foot
4 attending
5 interested in
6 operate
7 admission fee
8 describe

Conversation ❶

Concierge Service p.70

B Recommending restaurants

1 It's only a 10-minute walk from here.

2 Would you like me to make a reservation for you?

C Locating lost items

1 Can you describe what it looks like?
2 Let me get it from the back.

D Giving advice & directions for shopping

1 I need to buy some souvenirs for my family.
2 There are many street vendors at Namdaemun Market while there are many modern shopping malls at Dongdaemun Market.
3 Turn left as soon as you go through hotel's revolving door, and walk straight for about 5 minutes.
4 You'll see the subway station right in front of you.

Conversation ❷

GRO (Guest Relations Officer) Service p.73

B Handling requests from a VIP guest

1 Could you give me some details, please?
2 I'll need a conference room equipped with a videoconferencing system at 7:00 tomorrow morning.
3 Please make sure that there are toast, orange juice, and coffee.
4 I'll arrange a video conference for 7 o'clock tomorrow morning with five continental breakfasts.
5 Please let me know if you have any further requests.

C Giving directions to hotel facilities

1 Your conference will be held in the grand ballroom on the 2nd floor.
2 The conference is scheduled to start at 2 P.M.
3 Go straight toward the coffee shop.
4 Turn right and go to the end of the hall.
5 You can't miss it.

D Saying farewell to a guest

1 The rooms located on both ends of the corridor tend to be colder than the others.
2 I'll put a note on your profile so that you can get a room in the middle on your next visit.
3 Let me arrange a taxi and have a bellman put your baggage into the trunk while you settle the bill.

Exercises p.77

A

1 ⓑ
2 ⓒ
3 ⓒ
4 ⓐ

B

1 ⓐ
2 ⓔ
3 ⓑ
4 ⓒ
5 ⓓ

C

1 advice
2 visit
3 floor
4 open
5 admission

UNIT 07 Executive Floor

Warming Up p.80

B

ⓐ ☑
ⓑ ☑
ⓒ ☐
ⓓ ☑
ⓔ ☐
ⓕ ☑

Vocabulary p.81

1 take a seat
2 business card
3 explain
4 all-day
5 access
6 separate
7 along with
8 billed

Conversation I

EFL Check-In & Checkout Service p.82

B EFL checkout service

1 Can you prepare my bill while I am having breakfast?
2 Can you make two separate bills for me?
3 I will get your limo ready and have a bellman bring your baggage down to the car.

Conversation II

Lounge & Meeting Room Service p.84

B EFL meeting room service

1 I'd like to reserve a meeting room, please.
2 When would you like to use it?
3 It's available at that time.
4 How many people will be using the meeting room?
5 The meeting room is available free of charge for two hours per room.
6 Can you give me another person's name?
7 If you need anything else, please contact us on the executive floor.

Exercises p.87

A

1 ⓑ
2 ⓐ
3 ⓒ
4 ⓑ

B

1 ⓔ
2 ⓐ
3 ⓒ
4 ⓓ
5 ⓑ

C

1 hours
2 finished
3 refreshments
4 free of charge
5 place an order

08 Housekeeping

Warming Up
p.90

B

1 multi-adaptor
2 bandage
3 sewing kit
4 toilet paper

Vocabulary
p.91

1 out of order
2 allergic to
3 come in
4 deliver
5 hang up
6 stain

Conversation ❶
Making Up Rooms
p.92

B **Handling "Make Up Room" service requests**

1 Can you send someone to make up my room?
2 A maid will be there right away.
3 Can you also send me an iron and ironing board?
4 I'll have a maid bring them to you.
5 That's so kind of you.

C **Handling a turndown service request**

1 I forgot to take off the "Do Not Disturb" sign.
2 Can I get turndown service now?
3 I am allergic to feathers.
4 I will send someone with a nonallergenic foam pillow right away.
5 I'll send a maintenance man to your room right away.

Conversation ❷
Other Housekeeping Services
p.95

B **Handling lost and found items**

1 Do you remember your check-in date?

2 What does it look like?
3 It's made of white gold, and it has a crystal pendant.
4 We are keeping it at Housekeeping.
5 A receipt and an invoice will be sent to your email.

Exercises
p.97

A

1 ⓐ
2 ⓐ
3 ⓑ
4 ⓑ

B

1 ⓒ
2 ⓐ
3 ⓑ
4 ⓔ
5 ⓓ

C

1 Housekeeping
2 disturb
3 make up
4 nonallergenic
5 laundry

09 Hotel Facilities

Warming Up
p.100

B

1 swimming pool
2 gym
3 sauna
4 golf driving range

Vocabulary
p.101

1 overseas
2 fragile
3 copies
4 insurance
5 rent
6 staple

7 ⓐ   8 ⓗ

Delivering Room Service
p.115

B Handling mistakes

1 Could you set up a table over there, please?

2 Let me check your order slip.

3 I will be back to pick up the service cart in an hour.

Exercises
p.117

A

1 ⓒ   2 ⓑ
3 ⓐ   4 ⓑ

B

1 ⓒ   2 ⓐ
3 ⓑ   4 ⓔ
5 ⓓ

C

1 bowl

2 come with

3 Medium rare

4 out of

5 in season

UNIT 11 Restaurants & Bars

Warming Up
p.120

B

1 busboy

2 greeter

3 waiter/waitress

4 bartender

Vocabulary
p.121

1 ⓕ   2 ⓔ
3 ⓑ   4 ⓖ
5 ⓒ   6 ⓓ

Conversation Ⅰ

Reserving Tables & Greeting Customers
p.122

B Assigning a table for customers with a reservation

1 Under what name is it?

2 Where would you prefer to sit?

3 We have one in the corner. I will show you to your table.

4 Would you come this way, please?

5 How do you like this table?

C Assigning a table for walk-in customers

1 I'm afraid all our tables are taken.

2 Would you mind waiting until one is free?

3 Could you take a seat over there?

4 I'll call you when a table is ready.

5 I'm very sorry to have kept you waiting.

D At the Bar

1 Would you care for something to drink?

2 Would you like that straight up or on the rocks?

3 I would recommend a gin and tonic if you prefer a cocktail that isn't sweet.

Conversation Ⅱ

Taking Orders & Handling Payments
p.126

B Checking on diners

1 Enjoy your meal.

2 How is everything?

3 Would you like another glass of wine?

4 Could we have another round?

C Suggesting desserts

1 I'm sorry to interrupt.

2 May I take your plates?

3 Did you enjoy your meal?

4 I'm glad you liked the food.

5 Would you like some dessert?

D Handling payments

1   We would like to split the bill.

2   A 10% service charge is included in the bill.

3   Can I have your signature and room number here, please?

Exercises p.129

A

1   ⓑ   2   ⓐ
3   ⓐ   4   ⓐ

B

1   ⓔ   2   ⓓ
3   ⓑ   4   ⓒ
5   ⓐ

C

1   dine
2   taken
3   mind
4   seat
5   show

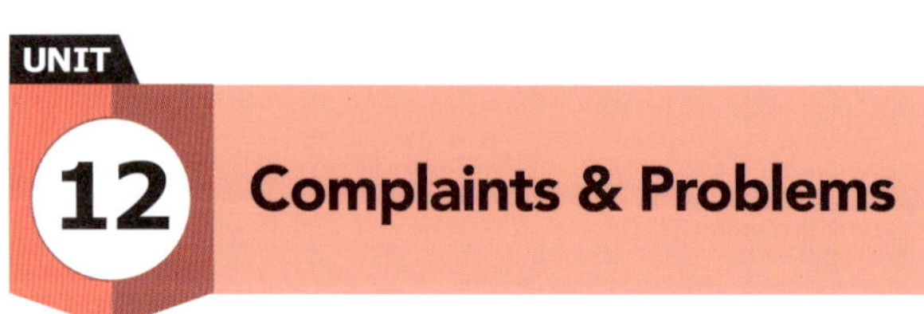

UNIT
12 Complaints & Problems

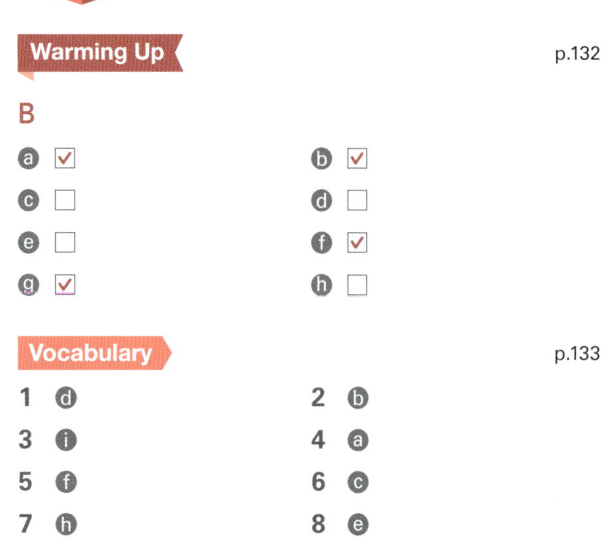

Warming Up p.132

B

ⓐ ☑   ⓑ ☑
ⓒ ☐   ⓓ ☐
ⓔ ☐   ⓕ ☑
ⓖ ☑   ⓗ ☐

Vocabulary p.133

1   ⓓ   2   ⓑ
3   ⓘ   4   ⓐ
5   ⓕ   6   ⓒ
7   ⓗ   8   ⓔ
9   ⓖ   10 ⓙ

Conversation ❶

Guest Complaints p.134

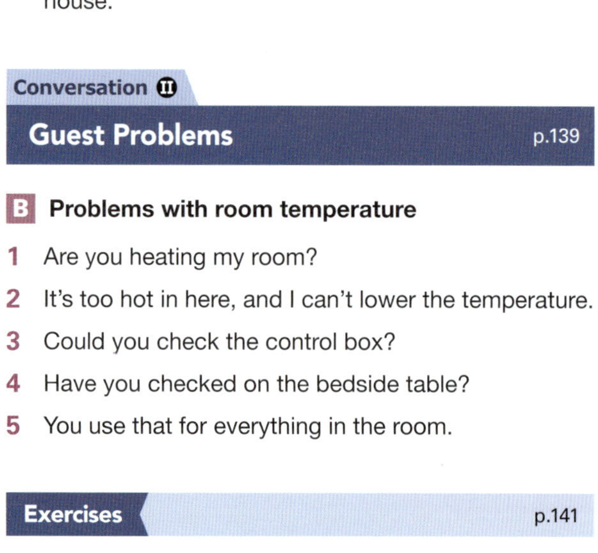

B Complaints about mischarges

1   Please check it over to see if there is anything wrong.

2   Let me check on the detailed bill.

3   I'm sorry for the inconvenience.

4   I will deduct them from your bill now.

C Complaints about the wrong room

1   I am afraid there must have been a mistake.

2   As a token of our apology, allow us to give you a complimentary bottle of wine.

D Complaints about restaurant service

1   What seems to be the problem?

2   I ordered my steak medium well done, but this steak is overcooked.

3   I'm terribly sorry that your steak is not cooked as you requested.

4   I'll take it back to the kitchen and have the chef cook a new one.

5   It will be ready in about 15 minutes.

6   Are there any other problems?

7   I will check on his order with the kitchen.

8   It has a lipstick stain on the rim.

9   I will replace it with a clean one right away.

10 Here are some desserts for you. They are on the house.

Conversation ❷

Guest Problems p.139

B Problems with room temperature

1   Are you heating my room?

2   It's too hot in here, and I can't lower the temperature.

3   Could you check the control box?

4   Have you checked on the bedside table?

5   You use that for everything in the room.

Exercises p.141

A

1   ⓑ   2   ⓒ

3 ⓐ   **4** ⓒ

1 ⓓ   **2** ⓐ

3 ⓔ   **4** ⓒ

5 ⓑ

1 ready

2 burned

3 apologize

4 replaced

5 token